THOMAS WHITESIDE

SELLING DEATH

Cigarette Advertising
and Public Health

LIVERIGHT/NEW YORK

Standard Book Number: 0-87140-541-5
Library of Congress Catalog Card Number: 75-162434

Designed by Paula Wiener
Manufactured in the United States of America

To Michael Pertschuk

Contents

SELLING DEATH

1

Introduction

In the sense that the product involved serves no valuable external function, is habituating to its consumers, and that use of it carries undesirable consequences the responsibility for which its manufacturers are heedless, the selling of cigarettes is symbolic of the mass merchandising of consumer products in this country. That is why, as someone who has done a considerable amount of writing on the subject of merchandising and the manipulation of consumers, I have been particularly interested for many years in the way in which cigarettes are advertised and marketed. Cigarette smoking is not a natural but an acquired habit, and getting people to acquire and maintain that habit, insofar as consumption of particular brands is concerned, has been an exercise into which the tobacco industry has poured many billions of dollars during the past half century.

As it happens, my opportunities to observe various aspects of the mass promotion of cigarettes stretch back to 1950, when I decided to do a reporting piece — it appeared in *The New Yorker* that summer — on the making of one of the cigarette commercials that were just beginning to appear on the television screen. At that time, the television networks hadn't developed to the point where they extended on a coast-to-coast basis; in fact, an executive in the advertising agency that I visited in the course of my reporting in 1950 seemed to find great wonder in revealing to me the statistic that in New York City in the evening more people were actually watching television than were listening to the radio.

The commercial I reported on was one for Lucky Strike cigarettes, and it was planned in the offices of the television department of Batten, Barton, Durstine & Osborn. The cigarette industry was probably the most eager of any section of business to get into television, and the tobacco companies were sponsoring such prime-time programs as "Arthur Godfrey and His Friends," "The Chesterfield Supper Club," "The Original Amateur Hour," "Stop the Music" and "Your Lucky Strike Theatre" — the latter produced by Robert Montgomery. Recently, in rereading the report that I wrote on the making of the Lucky Strike Commercial at B.B.D.O., what struck me most about it was part of a discussion I'd had with a Lucky Strike account executive named Jack Denove about the particular promise of the power of television to make smoking appear attractive to the consumer:

> I remarked to Denove that all the cigarette advertisements in print I could remember seeing showed people not smoking but merely holding lighted cigarettes, but that this principle didn't seem to apply to cigarette commercials on television. "No, it doesn't at all," he said. "They actually *smoke* them on television. You don't show people smoking

in still ads because the cigarette would hide the face. See what I mean?" Denove held one hand up to his mouth. "It doesn't look good, but smoking looks wonderful on television." Denove lit a Lucky, leaned back, and demonstrated the routine. "Look. You put your cigarette up to your face. You take your puff in the normal manner — watch me — and you blow out the smoke. It takes a couple of seconds. Then you see the person's face again. What could be more natural?"

Denove added, "We like everybody to both inhale *and* exhale on our commercials."

When one thinks, first, of the habituating effect of inhaling among smokers, and second, the carcinogenic effects of inhaling cigarette smoke as these have been demonstrated in extensive medical studies, the unique role of television advertising in the past twenty years in attracting potential smokers and conditioning them in what has been presented as a "natural" and socially acceptable and desirable habit is perhaps curiously foreshadowed in these remarks.

During those two decades, several billion dollars have been poured by the tobacco industry into television advertising, and a great deal of this money has been devoted in at least fifteen of those years to an attempt to offset or overwhelm news of statistical studies concerning the relationship between cigarette smoking and lung cancer, emphysema, heart disease, and other diseases. The conclusions of such studies began to come to public attention in the early fifties, and the answer of the tobacco industry to these developments was to promote the illusion of safety by the intensive advertising of filter brands. The proliferation of filter brands in the cigarette advertising business proved to be a bonanza for the cigarette companies and for the big Madison Avenue agencies.

As Rosser Reeves, the former chieftain of the Ted Bates agency, which was responsible for the hardest of the hard sell in advertising cigarettes, patent medicines, and other products on television in the fifties, put it to me some time ago in speaking of his advertising techniques,"It was just like wiring the slot machine to keep paying out a perpetual jackpot. My boy, it was like *printing money.*"

There was a time, before the results of studies on the ominous connection between cigarette smoking and illhealth and premature death began to make headlines in the press, during which one could understand how cigarette manufacturers could persuade themselves that smoking, while it didn't exactly improve people's health, was not the lethally dangerous habit it is now almost universally recognized to be — even though these manufacturers certainly were fully aware of the findings of Dr. E. Cuyler Hammond, who reported to the American Cancer Society in 1948 on the strong statistical connection between cigarette smoking and lung cancer in men, and similar and more detailed reports in the early fifties by Dr. Hammond and Dr. Daniel Horn in this country and by Drs. W.R. Doll and A.B. Hill in England. But by the early sixties, such a large body of authoritative studies showing clinical, epidemiological, chemical, and pathological evidence that cigarette smoking is a principal cause of lung cancer had accumulated that the case against cigarettes was by then an overwhelming one — so overwhelming that perhaps only tobacco manufacturers and their advertising agents could fail to grasp it. It was at that time, in 1963, that I set out to report, as soberly and fairly as I could, on the explanations or rationalizations of tobacco company executives and cigarette-account men in advertising agencies concerning their attitudes toward continuing to promote a product already widely recognized to be dangerous to human life. What they had to say was hardly encouraging to someone interested in the degree of social responsibility assumed within the structure of corporate power.

The now-famous report of the Advisory Committee of the Surgeon General, which was published in 1964, confirmed not only that cigarette smoking is a leading cause of lung cancer in males but also warned that "cigarette smoking is a health hazard of sufficient importance in the United States to warrant appropriate remedial action."

But that caused no appreciable change in the attitude of the corporate promoters of cigarettes concerning their responsibility to refrain from doing harm to public health. Lobbyists for the tobacco industry gutted the Cigarette Labelling and Advertising Bill of 1965, and turned the resulting Act into an instrument that effectively prevented federal regulatory agencies from requiring tobacco companies to include health warnings in their advertising for the next four years.

Before these preemptive provisions were to expire in June, 1969, I set out once more on an expedition into tobaccoland, to explore the lobbying of the tobacco interests on Capitol Hill on the Public Health Cigarette Smoking Act, and into the public relations antics of the Tobacco Institute, and the remarkable efforts on behalf of the public of a young lawyer, John F. Banzhaf III, who had succeeded in obtaining, under the Fairness Doctrine of the Federal Communications Commission, free time on television that enabled the American Cancer Society and the American Heart Association to warn the public daily on television, and in a very effective way, of the dangers to health and life itself of smoking.

The victory of the forces willing to put the cause of public health before the cause of corporate profits, represented in the passage of the Public Health Cigarette Smoking Act, is only a small step toward the control of public authority over the promotional excesses of the tobacco industry. It is plain that huge fortunes have been and are being made by the tobacco companies and Madison Avenue advertising agencies at the cost of immense human suffering, a great deal of which could certainly have been prevented long ago had the tobacco industry or their advertisers exerted control, or been made to exert control, over their overweening interest in corporate profits. If there were no profit to be made out of cigarettes, it would be remarkable to see how quickly the scales would fall from the eyes of the tobacco-industry executives, and how quickly they would be capable of seeing that cigarette smoking is, after all, a dangerous habit. However, the cigarette industry is wellknown among investors as a high-profit business, and even the ban on cigarette commercials on radio and television has failed to reduce the manufacturers' advertising campaigns, which have now been greatly extended in the printed media and on highway billboards. As this is written, at least one tobacco manu-facturing corporation is spending more money on advertising in print than it did when it was still pouring tens of millions of dollars annually into all the media, including television.

Thus, it seems quite clear that it is impossible to look for self-regulation by the cigarette industry over its advertising and promotional practices. Considering the annual toll in human lives from cigarette smoking, which on the basis of American Cancer Society estimates currently includes 45,000 deaths annually from lung cancer alone, there is no doubt that severe federal regulation of cigarette promotion is a most urgent necessity. And, as the reader of this book will observe, I am advocating, as a preliminary federal regulatory move, the immediate inclusion of cigarettes under the provisions of the Federal Hazardous Substances Act so that the U.S. government can be obliged, at long last, to act against the unregulated promotion of a product so demonstrably harmful to health.

May, 1971

2

A Cloud of Smoke

When a manufactured product that most consumers accept as useful or pleasurable comes under strong suspicion of being harmful to certain users, a number of acute problems confront the manufacturer. To solve them, he can do one of several things. If he is quite satisfied that his product presents no risk, he can do his best to reassure the public — and, if the sale of his product is subject to official regulation, the government — of its harmlessness. If he recognizes that a risk exists for certain users, he can try to modify his product, in order to render it as harmless as he knows how, or he can warn buyers of the nature of the risk, or he can withdraw the product from the market until its safety is firmly established. Whichever course he follows, the nature of the difficulty before him is not only technical and economic but moral. Such moral dilemmas are recurrent in American industry. At present, one of the most serious of them involves the tobacco business — the oldest industry in the country. During the past decade and a half, a number of medical people have produced an increasing weight of evidence showing that an association exists between people's smoking habits and the incidence of various diseases, including coronary heart disease, chronic bronchitis, emphysema, and lung cancer.

Of all the associations alleged to exist between smoking and disease, none has received more public attention than that between smoking and lung cancer. During the last half century, the annual death rate from all causes in this country has declined, but the death rate from lung cancer, once looked upon as a rare disease, is known to have increased strikingly. Between 1935 and 1962, deaths from lung cancer in the United States rose from four thousand to forty-one thousand, and while some of this increase is accounted for by population growth, the rate, standardized for age, is still about ten times what it was in the mid-thirties. Among men, who are seven times as likely to die of the disease as women, cancer of the lung has come to be the predominant form of fatal cancer in this country.

The extraordinary increase in the lung-cancer death rate first became the subject of intensive investigation among medical people in the late forties, and at that time (as subsequently) a number of possible causes were considered — among them the increase in various kinds of air pollution and the increase in the habit of cigarette smoking. The role of cigarette smoking attracted particular interest because of the rapid growth of the habit since the early part of the century, when most tobacco was smoked in pipes or chewed. Cigarettes became popular during the First World War, and between 1920 and 1948 the annual consumption of them rose from a rate of about seven hundred and fifty for each adult in the population to about twenty-four hundred. In 1949, Dr. E. Cuyler Hammond, reporting to the American Cancer Society on trends in cancer mortality, pointed to a strong statistical connection between heavy cigarette smoking and the incidence of lung cancer. Since then, scientific studies have been undertaken in various countries — the most elaborate of them in the United States being conducted by Dr. Hammond and Dr. Daniel Horn, and, in England, by Dr. W.R. Doll and Dr. A.B. Hill — and their principal result has been to implicate cigarette smoking as a factor intimately associated with lung cancer. In 1960, the Board of Directors of the American Cancer Society, having reviewed a number of these studies, gave as its judgment that "the clinical, epidemiological, experimental, chemical, and pathological evidence presented by the many studies reported in recent years indicates beyond reasonable doubt that cigarette smoking is the major cause of the unprecedented increase in lung cancer." In 1962, the Royal College of Physicians, in Britain, issued an extensive review of the subject. It concluded that "cigarette smoking is the most likely cause of the worldwide increase in deaths from lung cancer," and that the habit probably also contributed to the development of coronary heart disease, chronic bronchitis, and lesser diseases. Both societies have asserted that while lung cancer is rare among nonsmokers — and almost nonexistent among non-smokers in rural areas — it is less rare among cigar and pipe smokers, and its incidence among cigarette smokers varies in direct ratio to the number of cigarettes smoked and the amount of smoke inhaled. And both organizations have concluded that ordinary urban air pollution seems to be a comparatively minor factor in the incidence of lung cancer, although the disease can be induced by prolonged exposure to certain industrial dusts and fumes. According to a summary made by the American Cancer Society earlier this year, the death rate from lung cancer — death certificates being taken at face value — is seven times as great for people who smoke less than half a pack a day as it is for nonsmokers, while for those who smoke two or more packs a day, it is more than twenty times as great.

As a consequence of these and other assertions, which were accompanied by widespread publicity, the American tobacco industry has had to cope with a lot of trouble. The trouble began to be very noticeable in 1953. In that year, the *Journal of the American Medical Association* carried an article by Dr. Alton Ochsner — a physician who had been warning his colleagues for at least seventeen years of a suspicious relationship between smoking and lung cancer — in which he flatly called smoking a principal cause of the disease. Also in that year, an article appeared in *Cancer Research* reporting on the results of a study of the possible carcinogenic effects of tobacco smoke by Dr. Ernest L. Wynder and Dr. Evarts Graham, who concluded that cancer could be induced on the skin of mice by tobacco-tar condensates, and yet another article, entitled "Cancer by the Carton," appeared in *Reader's Digest*. Following this publicity, cigarette sales declined for the first time in twenty-one years. The situation was perturbing enough to induce the major tobacco manufacturing and handling companies to take full-page display ads in the press at the beginning of 1954; these announced that the industry, while it had full confidence that its products were not injurious to health, was "pledging aid and assistance to the research effort into all phases of tobacco use and health," and had set up a Tobacco Industry Research Committee, to be directed by "a scientist of unimpeachable integrity and national repute," which would have available the services of "an Advisory Board of scientists disinterested in the cigarette industry." The scientific director appointed was Dr. Clarence Cook Little, an eminent geneticist and cancer specialist, who was then director of the Roscoe B. Jackson Memorial Laboratory, at Bar Harbor, Maine, and who had formerly been managing director of the American Society for Control of Cancer, the predecessor of the American Cancer Society. Since its formation, the Tobacco Industry Research Committee has spent over six million dollars, contributed by tobacco manufacturers, for the support of research by various medical groups into various aspects of smoking and cancer and other diseases. In the nearly ten years that the committee has been at work, Dr. Little has consistently maintained that the relationship between smoking and health has been insufficiently investigated and is too complex to warrant a conclusion that smoking is a cause of lung cancer or of other diseases; that it remains to be seen whether genetic, hormonal, emotional, or other differences between smokers and nonsmokers — as well as differences in their external environment — afford clues to their differing health risks; and that the cause of lung cancer, as of cancer in general, is still unknown.

Several eminent medical men agree with Dr. Little. However, various governments abroad have considered the weight of the evidence associating cigarette smoking with lung cancer so impressive that they have adopted a policy of discouraging cigarette smoking, especially among younger people. In Britain, where the lung-cancer death rate is even higher than in the United States, the Ministry of Health, acting on a recommendation of the Royal College of Physicians, began an extensive publicity campaign to warn people that cigarette smoking is dangerous to health, and so far about a million posters — a typical one entitled "Before You Smoke, THINK: Cigarettes Cause Lung Cancer" — have been distributed to British schools, clinics, and post offices, and put up in various public places. As a result of the government's approach to the problem, the Independent Television Authority, the group that governs commercial television in Britain, came to an agreement with British cigarette manufacturers to restrict the showing of cigarette commercials to the hours after 9 P.M., in order to minimize children's exposure to them. In Canada, too, after the Canadian Medical Association issued a report that characterized cigarette smoking as "a grave and extensive health problem," cigarette commercials have been voluntarily restricted to late-evening hours. Various restrictions on cigarette advertising have been put into effect by the governments of West Germany and Denmark, and even the Soviet Union has mounted a poster campaign asserting that smoking is an unhealthy habit. In the United States, the American Medical Association has not yet taken an official stand on the nature of the association between smoking and lung cancer. Nor has the United States government. But in October of 1962, largely as a result of a letter sent to the President jointly by the American Cancer Society, the American Heart Association, the American Public Health Association, and the National Tuberculosis Association asking that a committee be appointed to examine "the social responsibilities" of business and government in protecting the health of the public, the Surgeon General of the United States Public Health Service announced that he had appointed an Advisory Committee on Smoking and Health to "make a comprehensive review of all available data on smoking and other factors in the environment that may affect health." This review, he said, would be followed by recommendations for action, if necessary. [The study was published in January, 1964.]

The American cigarette industry, while it has suffered some hard blows, has by no means been laid low by them. If one were to match the weight of all the unfavorable publicity about smoking against the weight of cigarette advertising campaigns, advertising and smoking would unquestionably triumph. The initial drop in cigarette sales has long since been recovered. Since 1953, the number of cigarettes smoked in this country in a year has risen from three hundred and eighty-seven billion to more than half a trillion. Only part of this increase can be accounted for by the expansion of the population; on an adult per-capita basis, the figures rose from 3,559 cigarettes in 1953 to 4,005 in 1963. In England, cigarette sales dipped about four percent in the year following the Royal College report on smoking, but the drop has since been recovered and the English tobacco manufacturers were by 1963 selling more cigarettes than ever. As for the American cigarette industry, its prosperity, whatever its difficulties, is greater than at any other period in its history.

In growing to its present state of affluence, the industry has undergone considerable changes in its patterns of cigarette merchandising over the last few years. The most noticeable changes have been, of course, the introduction of many new brand names and the rise in the popularity of filter cigarettes. Twenty years ago, there were five big brands — Lucky Strike, Camel, Chesterfield, Old Gold, and Philip Morris — which accounted for ninety-five percent of all cigarette sales in the country. By 1960 fifteen brands accounted for roughly the same percentage. The large cigarette companies of that day and this — R.J.Reynolds, American Tobacco, Liggett & Myers, Philip Morris, P. Lorillard, and Brown & Williamson — are now manufacturing fifty-one different brands, in sixty-nine sizes and packages. The familiarity of some brand names, like Philip Morris and Old Gold, has faded in the public consciousness; now the big names include Kent, Winston, Marlboro, and L & M, and nobody can get through an evening of television without encountering showers of commercials for such newer brands as Newport, Salem, Spring, Montclair, Belair, and Alpine. Among these newer brands, the majority are filter cigarettes of one length or another. The filter has perhaps been the principal merchandising device used by tobacco manufacturers in their attempt to reassure smokers about possible health hazards. In the early fifties, filter cigarettes constituted barely one percent of all cigarettes sold; now they account for almost fifty-five percent. Presumably, the function of a filter is to trap condensates — including nicotine and the so-called tars — from the smoke of a cigarette. The first filter cigarette to be promoted here in a big way was Kent, which was put on the market, at a premium price, by Lorillard, the makers of Old Gold, in 1952. At the time, the only other filter cigarettes were Brown & Williamson's Viceroy, which had a crêpe-paper filter, and Benson & Hedges' Parliament, which had a filter packed with a tuft of cotton. Lorillard, which had been failing with Old Gold and needed something new, introduced

Kent with a great fanfare over its "exclusive Micronite filter," made of stuff that had been "developed by researchers in atomic-energy plants." In 1953, when the question of smoking and health had become a matter of general public discussion, the prospects for Kent, helped along by hygienic-sounding advertising about the material in the Micronite filter ("so safe, so pure, it's used to filter the air in leading hospitals"), looked promising to its makers. But Kent sales slumped not long thereafter, partly because many smokers found it so hard to draw smoke through the filter that they scarcely had the sensation of smoking at all. Nevertheless, Lorillard's competitors were all hard at work on filter cigarettes of their own. Brown & Williamson put new infusions of advertising money into promoting its Viceroy. Philip Morris not only bought out Benson & Hedges in order to get the cotton-filtered Parliament but proceeded to develop a filter cigarette of its own from one of its old properties, Marlboro. Reynolds, the makers of Camel, came along with Winston. American Tobacco, which already had the cork-tipped, king-size Herbert Tareyton, now dressed it up with a "new Selective Filter," featuring "an entirely new concept in cigarette filtration – a filter tip of purified cellulose, incorporating *Activated Charcoal*, a filtering substance world famous as a purifying agent." Liggett & Myers put out L & M, with a "Pure White Miracle Tip of Alpha-Cellulose" ("Just what the doctor ordered"). By 1955, the filter boom was on in earnest, with each tobacco company striving to outdo the others in claims for the efficiency of its particular filters. It was the beginning of an era known in the business as the Tar Derby. The boom was a great gift to the industry in that it counteracted many of the injurious effects that publicity about smoking and health had been having on sales. It was also a gift to the industry in that while most of the manufacturers charged premium prices for filter cigarettes, the filters actually cost less to produce than the tobacco they displaced. The filters used in some brands were capable of reducing, to some extent, the amount of tar and nicotine normally inhaled per cigarette, but the ones used in several other brands, in spite of their loudly proclaimed merits, weren't. According to Dr. Hammond, some of the filters actually strained out less tar and nicotine than the tobacco they displaced would have done. Furthermore, as time went on, most of the tobacco manufacturers compensated for the filter's reduction of flavor by packing their cigarettes with stronger-flavored grades of tobacco, some of which had a higher tar and nicotine content than before. Also, as time went on, they added, for reasons of economy, "reconstituted" or "homogenized" material, including tobacco remnants that in less efficient days would have been discarded. And, in order to let the customer know that he was indeed smoking a cigarette, several of the manufacturers began loosening up their filters. The net result of such changes was that smokers who switched from regular cigarettes to filters in the belief that they were reducing the risk to their health were sometimes exposing themselves to greater amounts of tar and nicotine than ever. (To take a couple of examples derived from a report published in 1958 by a congressional investigating committee and based on laboratory tests conducted by Consumers Union: A smoker of Lorillard's Old Gold who in 1953 switched to Lorillard's Kent in order to cut down on tar and nicotine would have accomplished his aim in that year, but by 1957, if he was still smoking Kent, he would have been inhaling, through the atomic-age Micronite filter, six percent more tar and twenty-six percent more nicotine per cigarette than he had inhaled when he smoked Old Gold in 1953; in the intervening years, Lorillard, to increase sales of Kent, had loosened the Micronite filter. Again, if a 1955 smoker of Reynolds' Camel switched to the same company's Winston, he would have found that in 1957 he was taking in sixteen percent more nicotine and twenty-three percent more tar than he had been with Camel. Of course, it might be argued that a Winston, being king-size and considerably longer than a Camel, would contain more tobacco, and hence more nicotine and tar, but in 1956 the president of Reynolds conceded to a Senate-House committee that a Winston actually contained eight percent less tobacco than a Camel. In any case, it should be added that today the tar-and-nicotine content of all cigarettes – filtered and unfiltered – has been markedly lowered.)

The furious Tar Derby reached its climax in 1960, when the Federal Trade Commission, which hitherto had had little success in trying to get the tobacco manufacturers to moderate their claims for filter cigarettes, put its foot down and announced that no more tar-and-nicotine claims would be permitted in cigarette advertising, and that the tobacco companies had made a "voluntary" agreement to this effect. Since that time, cigarette advertising has carried on without making specific, as distinct from implied, claims about the effectiveness of filters. Nowadays, most of the overt claims made about the advantages of particular cigarettes revolve around considerations that are entirely subjective and beyond the reach of measure – considerations of "taste," "flavor," "mildness," and the like. Yet the issue of health seems to underlie cigarette advertising as strongly today as it ever did during the Tar Derby. In their glow of supreme physical well-being, the models in the cigarette ads — whether the man and the girl snuggling up to each other on the deck of a yacht and lighting up each other's Tareytons ("The Tareyton ring marks the real thing") or the champion water skier celebrating an exhibition of his skill by puffing away at a Camel ("Every inch a real smoke") — certainly seem to be living refutations of any theory that smoking might have something unhealthy about it. In the last few years, smoking — and romance between smoking couples — seems to have moved outdoors from more stuffy surroundings. This impression is reinforced by the ads for menthol-flavored cigarettes. Since 1957 or so, menthol cigarettes have become the fastest-growing segment of the business. They have been promoted for their "cool" or "fresh" taste, and the millions of smokers who have switched to them — partly, perhaps, in the understandable, if mistaken, belief that their smoke is somehow cleaner than that of other cigarettes — may have had this belief strengthened by gazing at some of the countless television commercials and four-color ads showing couples plunging in and out of the surf on Caribbean-looking shores ("Newport smokes fresher") or dallying by waterfalls or covered bridges surrounded by delicate greenery ("It's springtime every time you light up a Salem!"). And as the cigarette-ad models seem to have taken en masse to fresh air (in some commercials air itself seems to have become almost a commodity — as in Salem's claim that "Salem's high-porosity paper air-softens every puff"), so do they seem to have acquired the habit of inhaling. Fifteen years ago, when network television was just getting started and visual cigarette advertising was pretty much confined to the printed media, tobacco ads did not even go so far as to show the models in the act of smoking, let alone inhaling; the cigarettes were merely held near the mouth. In the early television commercials, some of the girl models, while they were smokers, all right, didn't really inhale and weren't required to blow much smoke around. Now the tobacco companies require as a matter of course that models be able to inhale properly, and even the youngest-looking of the girls seem to be able to do so pretty deeply. (Dr. Hammond, in an article surveying a number of studies on smoking and health: "In relation to total death rates, the degree of inhalation is as important, perhaps more important, than the amount of smoking.") While specific claims about the value of filters in dissipating the effects of inhaling may be taboo, the filters themselves are very much in evidence in cigarette ads and commercials. Whatever uneasiness about his habit may lie in the mind of a smoker, he can always look to the ads for some kind of reassurance, and no doubt somewhere he can find it. A Parliament smoker, for example, might take comfort in hearing and seeing in commercial after commercial that "Parliament gives you Extra Margin." He can have little doubt that the Extra Margin is essentially one of safety, even though the word "safety" is never mentioned; Parliament commercials with the "Extra Margin" theme are keyed to activities that involve physical danger, such as speedboat racing, parachute jumping, bobsledding, and ice hockey, and the viewer is led to equate the cigarette with such safety devices as protective goggles, crash helmets, and life preservers. However, if Parliament with its recessed filter is indeed something like a life preserver, Parliament advertising is silent on the nature of any danger that the smoker is being preserved against. That issue is clouded in smoke, perhaps very like the smoke called for in a recent "story board," or illustrated script for a proposed Parliament commercial. A boy and a girl, looking happy and secure with the Extra Margins of seat belts and Parliaments, are jolting along in a jeep over sand dunes:

> THEY LAUGH AS THEY SMOKE, CUT TO HER REACT-
> ING: LAUGHS AS SHE TAKES IN DEEP, DELICIOUS
> DRAG ON CIGARETTE. STAY ON HER AS SHE RE-
> MOVES CIG ... LOOKS AT FILTER WITH QUIET AP-
> PROVAL. CUT TO HIM FAST. HE BLOWS OUT SMOKE
> SO YOU KNOW HE THINKS PARLIAMENTS ARE
> GREAT.

The scale on which cigarette advertising is conducted is enormous and is expanding steadily. During the last ten years, the tobacco companies have increased their annual expenditures on television commercials from forty million dollars in 1957 to about a hundred and fifteen million dollars in 1962, and as the number of brands on the market has increased, so has the competition between them — a struggle in which battalions of water skiers, airplane pilots, and speedboat racers are deployed to overwhelm the opposition and assure the fidelity of the public to a particular brand. A good deal of earnest conferring among the strategists of the tobacco wars involves considerations of "brand loyalty" and "brand image." The creation of a brand image involves the manufacture and assembly of prepackaged elements of a sort of daydream — a set of visual and aural associations that will be launched from Madison Avenue into the minds of scores of millions of actual and potential smokers, there to be kept orbiting incessantly around the periphery of consciousness. "Tremendous loyalties are built up for a product as personal as a cigarette," the vice-president of an advertising agency in charge of a big cigarette account says. "The food a man eats, the toothpaste he uses, the socks he wears are all pretty personal matters to him, but none of these things tend to be as personal to him as the cigarette he smokes. It attaches a tremendous personal significance. He has it on display all day long. He has it on his person. He has it in his mouth. He draws its smoke into his lungs. It is safe to say that many cigarettes have a satisfactory taste, but the principal thing is the personal identification with the brand."

A good example of the creation of a brand image occurred in the promotion of Philip Morris's Marlboro filter cigarette. It was introduced into the cigarette market on a national scale in 1955, when the filter boom was just getting under way. At that time, the use of filter cigarettes was still associated to a considerable extent with women. Furthermore, Marlboro itself, up to then, had been a woman's cigarette, available with either an ivory or a ruby tip, but no filter. When the Philip Morris people decided to go into the filter business, they picked the Marlboro name, with the help of market research, as a promising one, and then abandoned the old brand except for the name. In promoting the new filter Marlboro, they resolved to strike at the prevailing notion that "there was something sissy about smoking filter cigarettes," as a Philip Morris executive recently put it. "We decided to go in for male-oriented imagery," he said. The result was a barrage of Marlboro ads showing the filter brand being smoked by determined-looking males with tattoos on their arms. "The image of the Marlboro man that we projected was one of the successful, up-the-hard-way sort of guy, who got himself tattooed somewhere along the line," the same Philip Morris executive said. "Gray, mature, rugged — the wealthy-rancher type rather than the Arrow Collar type. The brand personality of Marlboro was altogether different from the personality of, say, our Parliament, which was a sort of friendly, gregarious spirit — a fella-and-girl kind of warmth. The Marlboro approach has been a kind of male, mood thing. Marlboro advertising uses women only secondarily. On TV, we do use Julie London — she sits and sings the Marlboro Song, 'You Get a Lot to Like with a Marlboro,' to a guy in a night club or in the back seat of a limousine — but, generally speaking, the Marlboro man is *alone*. He is reflective as he relaxes with the cigarette. There is masculinity, and I would even say moodiness, rather than just mood — although not fickle moodiness. This brand personality is very important to us. The consumer who lights up the product — we've conditioned him. We've told him what kind of product he's got." Within two or three years after its introduction, Marlboro, pushed by vigorous advertising campaigns, became one of the best-selling filter cigarettes on the market. And, thanks to a big chunk of the thirty million dollars that Philip Morris is estimated to spend annually on advertising, it still is. In an average week, perhaps ninety million people could be exposed to Marlboro — or, in the language of Madison Avenue, "delivered" to the advertisers, at a certain cost per thousand viewers.

For all the manipulative air of such talk, it would be quite incorrect to assume that any given force of advertising automatically assures a given degree of success in persuading the public to buy a particular brand of cigarette. Of the fourteen new brands that the tobacco companies have introduced with extensive advertising and on a national scale in the early Sixties, very few have been taken up by the smoking public in a way that their manufacturers have considered satisfactory. The marketplace has been littered with what the merchandisers sadly refer to as "brand failures" — makes with names like Hit Parade, Brandon, Oasis, and Duke of Durham. "You never can count on what's going to happen when you introduce a brand, even with the best planning," a tobacco executive has said. "Let's say you see a niche in the market for a new product and you think you can put out something that will fill it. You go to your experts, who come up with acceptable combinations of tobacco blends and filters. You test these out on consumer panels, just as you do everything else — the color of the package, the design, the brand names you have in mind, and so on — and eventually you start manufacture and put the product on sale in a regional test market. You ask yourself questions: Is the media weight you're putting behind it sufficient? Is this an item acceptable to the retailers? Is it going to get repeats — you're getting the tryers, but are they coming back? Is the taste of the product more satisfying? You listen to consumer reaction — to the things they play back to you. If you have a package innovation, is that playing back? How much do you need to remold your advertising to fit the things that play back? You need the answers to these and other questions before you make a commitment to go national. If you get a positive answer, you put it in the corporate mix and you're ready to go. Once you've committed yourself to going national, you've committed yourself to a multimillion-dollar decision."

The introduction of new and competing brands of cigarettes on a national scale resembles a game of chance in which the ante required for each player begins at something like eight million dollars and playing the game itself can be far more costly than that; the American Tobacco Company is estimated to have put between twenty and thirty million dollars into the promotion of its Hit Parade brand before it gave it up as a lost cause. However, the possible winnings are enough to insure no shortage of players, and hardly a season passes without the entry of some new brand from the test markets into the arena of full-scale national promotion. The competition being what it is, the contenders seldom pass up an opportunity to seize on a promotional point that they think may give them an edge, however slight, on their opponents – whether the edge is a newly coined word for a filter or some hygienic-looking set of surroundings for the television-commercial models to smoke in. Cigarette merchandisers are constantly concerned with "dimensions of difference" ("At that time, the brand's dimension of difference was provided by the flip-top box") and "product differences" ("Then Newport came along and added 'A Hint of Mint' and that was the product difference"). During 1963 no fewer than three new filter brands – Montclair, Paxton, and Lark – were shot out of the corporate mix and into the national market, and their promoters have made the most of whatever differences exist between them. Montclair, with a "unique development in compound filters," is the only cigarette that "puts the menthol in the filter, where it cannot burn" and "makes the last puff taste as fresh as the first puff." Paxton, the "first menthol cigarette to meet the challenge of today's smoking needs," features a "new Humiflex pack" and a "new team of filters back to back," one of the filters being "fortified with Pecton." Lark features a "three-piece Keith filter" that contains "two modern outer filters plus an inner filter of charcoal granules — a basic material science uses to purify air."

What impurities, if any, these and other such portentously described filtering devices are actually supposed to filter out remains unexplained in the ads. In fact, it is difficult to find a tobacco manufacturer who will concede that cigarettes contain anything impure enough to require filtering out at all.

The fact that the tobacco industry never deals overtly in its advertising with the issue of smoking and health does not mean that it has no pronouncements to make on the subject. Most of its pronouncements are issued by the Tobacco Institute, Inc., a trade organization that was formed by the major tobacco manufacturers in 1958 to look after some of their common interests. (It is independent of Dr. Little's Tobacco Industry Research Committee.) The Tobacco Institute, which has its headquarters in Washington, is headed by George V. Allen, the former director of the United States Information Agency, and Mr. Allen, in speeches before various organizations, has set forth its position by saying that the answers to questions about smoking and health are unknown, that the whole subject remains a speculative one, and that while some statistical studies have pointed the way to further research, they have not provided answers to the original questions. "We are not on a crusade either for or against tobacco," Allen has been quoted as saying. "If we have a crusade, it is a crusade for research." During the pursuit of such research, he has called for a "respite from theories, resolutions, and emotional statements" about smoking and health. The Tobacco Institute, in fact, is quite vocal on the subject of research, and, with the help of Hill & Knowlton, a big public-relations outfit with headquarters in New York, it sends more than a hundred thousand physicians around the country a quarterly publication called *Tobacco and Health Research*, a summary and compendium of items having to do with research on these subjects. The items are presented under such headings as "Autopsy Study Fails to Support Smoking Tie to Vascular Ills," "Lung Cancer Deaths 20% Overstated," and "Experts Differ on Royal College Report."

Besides pointing out to doctors what it considers the statistical fallacies and misconceptions in the studies that have drawn a causal connection between smoking and certain diseases, the Institute has had to contend with public criticism not only of the industry's own use of statistics in the past ("More Doctors Smoke Camels Than Any Other Cigarette") but of the manner in which it has continued to promote its products, particularly among young people. In England, the advertising of cigarettes on commercial television — as here, the principal medium used — is governed by a quite elaborate set of "guidance notes," drawn up by the television companies and subscribed to by the tobacco manufacturers. They provide, among other things, that "advertisements should not encourage people, and young people in particular, to believe that they will have any advantage romantically, physically, socially, or in their jobs if they smoke." Among the specific appeals to be avoided are:

"Hero appeal" and the appeal to "manliness."
The appeal of social success, or the suggestion that

smoking is part of the modern, smart, sophisticated, or fashionable way of life . . . .

The creation of a romantic atmosphere in which it is implied that cigarettes are an essential ingredient.

An impression of exaggerated satisfaction; e.g., deep inhaling or expressions of intense enjoyment associated with smoking.

The use in advertisements of young people *unmistakably* under the age of twenty-one.

The suggestion that cigarettes overcome "nerves" or strain, [or are] an aid to relaxation or concentration.

Nothing like this set of restraints has existed in cigarette advertising on television here, of course, and nothing remotely as thoroughgoing seems to have been urged upon the American tobacco industry or the television broadcasters by their critics. However, in November, 1962, LeRoy Collins, the former Governor of Florida and the president of the National Association of Broadcasters, who has the reputation of being a maverick in the broadcasting business, made a speech before a group of broadcasters in Portland, Oregon, in which he suggested that, because of what he called "mounting evidence that tobacco provides a serious hazard to health," broadcasters had a moral responsibility to consider taking "corrective action" against the televising of some types of cigarette commercials, notably those featuring well-known athletes and those expressly designed to influence young people. The reaction of the broadcasting industry to Collins' remarks was not at all favorable, and for a while there was talk that Collins would be asked to resign from his job. Nonetheless, his speech did have the effect of stirring up questions about the wisdom of aiming cigarette advertising at young people, and in June, 1962, the Tobacco Institute, responding to this pressure, issued a statement declaring that the tobacco industry had always taken the position that "smoking is a custom for adults," and that, in conformity with this belief, a number of companies had decided to discontinue advertising in college publications and engaging in other campus promotional activities. For years, most of the tobacco companies had been conducting campaigns to persuade college students to smoke their particular brands, both through placing advertising in college publications (the cigarette industry became the biggest single source of revenue for many such publications) and through the promotional activities of paid "campus representatives" among the student body, to whom they gave quantities of sample packs for free distribution.

The Institute's declaration that smoking was "a custom for adults," and thus, presumably, not one for non-adults, did have one result that applied on a broader basis than merely the college-publication level. In the fall of 1963, the American Tobacco Company began an extensive campaign for Lucky Strike cigarettes in which the advertising copy contained the statement that "smoking is a pleasure meant for adults." This sentiment appeared under a headline, spread over two pages, that asserted, "Lucky Strike Separates the Men from the Boys . . . But Not from the Girls." On the left-hand page, the first part of the headline was illustrated by a photograph of a helmeted, Lucky Strike-smoking racing-car driver who was smilingly flourishing a winner's cup as he received the adulatory glances of youths pressing close behind him; on the right-hand page, the second part of the headline was illustrated by a shot of the same model — still equipped with his cigarette, smile, and cup but minus the young male fans — being hugged by a girl admirer. However, the ad men, having ostensibly set out to illustrate the theme that cigarettes are not for boys, thus achieved just the opposite effect by making the smoking of Lucky Strike appear to be the act that turns a boy into a man. But such mistakes can happen in cigarette advertising. It is even possible that they will happen more frequently in the future. With the growth rate of the cigarette market slowing down and the competition between manufacturers becoming increasingly heavy, there is really only one way for the industry to maintain its rate of expansion, and that is by doing business with the great mass of young people who reach smoking age each year. This is a potential market that is literally getting bigger by the minute. Over the past decade, the number of people between eighteen and twenty-four in this country increased by only two percent, owing to the low birth rate of the Depression years, but over the next decade their number, owing to the high birth rate of the postwar boom period, will increase by fifty-two percent. And in the young-adult population bulge the eighteen-year-olds of 1966 were the fifteen-year-olds of 1963, as this chapter was written. As these fifteen-year-olds were maturing, so was the tobacco for them to smoke, as it lay waiting in millions of hogsheads in the curing warehouses of the tobacco manufacturers.

Because of my interest in the dilemma confronting the tobacco industry, and because it seemed to me too bad that, owing to the relative anonymity of so many of the responsible people in the industry, their personal views on the issue of smoking and health — as distinct from the formally phrased announcements issued on their collective behalf — should be so little known, I set out recently to interview several people who are concerned with the merchandising of cigarettes. While I cannot say that there was any great eagerness to see me and talk about this touchy subject, I must say that when I was received, it was always with great courtesy and attentiveness.

My first call was upon James C. Bowling, who is assistant to Joseph F. Cullman III, the president of Philip Morris, Inc., at the Philip Morris headquarters on Park Avenue — a very smart set of offices. Bowling is a well-dressed, round-faced man in his middle thirties who talks smoothly and equably in a southern accent. He has spent all his working life with Philip Morris. Even when he was attending the University of Louisville, he worked for the company as a campus representative, and after his graduation he worked for it as a tobacco salesman and then as a supervisor of campus representatives, making his way up through the ranks to his present position. Bowling was smoking from a pack of his company's new Paxton cigarettes — the ones with the team of filters back to back — and, like every other executive I encountered, he seemed to smoke almost incessantly. I asked him for his views on the connection that has been said to exist between smoking and disease, and he told me that, like all his colleagues, he had given the matter a good deal of serious thought. "We believe that there is no connection, or we wouldn't be in the business," he said earnestly, and, in a phrase that was to become familiar to me, he went on the characterize the issue as "the health scare." "I remember a speaker last year at the three hundred and fiftieth anniversary celebration of America's first tobacco crop at Jamestown telling of the trials that the tobacco industry had at that time," he said. "They had a health scare at the inception of the industry in America. And the scare goes further back than that — King James issued his 'Counterblaste to Tobacco' in 1604. We've had these trials from time to time, and each time the industry has come through stronger, because people have demonstrated conclusively that they want to smoke. When the health scare hit in 1952 or '53, we were all staggered, though. The matter was put forward not as a thesis but as an absolute fact. Yet it was clear to us — and to a few eminent statisticians, like the late Sir Ronald Fisher — that the case was far from proved, and the industry did the correct thing by taking the attitude that nothing could or should be done until the facts were in. The work of the Tobacco Industry Research Committee has been under way for ten years, and it has required a great deal of restraint not to lash back at the anti-cigarette forces. The people on the T.I.R.C. are eminent people. We in the industry have no contact with them, but we read all we can about the research they're doing. Everybody in the industry has been forced to become an authority in his peer group on the subject. It's impossible for me, for example, to go somewhere without meeting someone who wants to talk about it. I wonder how many conversations about it take place without a full understanding of the facts. Gosh, we're awed at how a story can be told and retold by the anti-cigarette people, and how little attention is given in the press to claims *for* cigarettes. But I'm also impressed with the way many people are sifting the facts for themselves and coming up with the conclusion that the case against tobacco is not proved."

Bowling lit up another Paxton and went on, "It surprises people sometimes that we should take it so seriously. I don't know why we should take it lightly. I'm from Kentucky, and I know what tobacco has meant to that one state. Some people who attack the industry don't stop to think that we're *people* — and people with a social conscience. Just as I feel I'm personally committed in this business, so do other people. I don't know of one executive who has resigned as a result of the health scare. The purveyors of pleasure-feeling may have been put in some jeopardy by the attacks of the anti-cigarette people, and the attacks may have made us more than a trifle self-conscious, but we believe that we're right, and that history will show this to be so. Meanwhile, people are smoking and enjoying it. An eminent physician sat in the chair you're sitting in not so long ago, and he said that if people were to stop smoking, there had better be something pretty powerful to take its place or there would be more wife-beating and job dissatisfaction than people's natures could tolerate."

From Bowling's office I went on to see John T. Landry, a tall, clear-faced, curly-haired man who, at thirty-nine, is the company's director of brand management, which means that he is responsible for the advertising of all its brands. Landry came to Philip Morris in 1956; previously, he had been the advertising manager for the Blue Coal Corporation, in New York, and before that he was in the advertising-research department of *Newsweek*. He made it clear to me that he really enjoyed being in the tobacco business. "It's hectic, it's competitive, and there are a lot of easier ways to live, but it's a great business," he said. "It's a real big business." Although Landry had a pack of Paxtons on his desk, the cigarette he was smoking was a Marlboro. The executive in charge of the promotion of a particular brand of cigarette is expected to smoke that brand, but Landry, being in charge of all Philip Morris's brands, could smoke any of them with propriety, and he told me that his personal preference was for Marlboro. After some discussion of brand promotion, I brought the conversation around to the issue of smoking and health. "We all assume that, as Mr. Cullman, the president of our company, said at the last annual meeting, cigarettes will ultimately be exonerated," Landry told me with conviction. "We all feel that way or we wouldn't be selling them. We're parents, citizens, members of society, you know. This business has been a respectable business for hundreds of years. I frequently get asked by people I come across about my attitude toward cigarettes. I've seen our research facilities in Richmond, and I know that other companies have facilities just as big, and up to this point nobody has ever shown anything conclusive about cigarettes and health — lung cancer and all that. It just hasn't been proved. I think if it were proved I would give up smoking. I also think I'd get the heck out of the business. Not because the business would be hurt but because I would not like to sell a product that was harmful. Even now, I wouldn't try to convince anyone that cigarettes are physically good for him, but from an emotional point of view smoking eases tension, and if I didn't smoke I'd probably develop a tic or something. My wife smokes, I smoke, and we certainly don't have any fear of it. I don't think that cigarettes will ever be found to contain anything dangerous to health. The problem is being worked on, and in the meantime I am very happy in this business."

From the offices of Philip Morris I went to those of Benton & Bowles, the advertising agency that prepares the ads for about half of the company's products, where I had an appointment with Henry Pattison, the chairman of the agency's executive committee. Pattison, who has direct charge of the Philip Morris account, is a highly experienced advertising man, and has been with Benton & Bowles in an executive role for more than twenty years. He is a big man in his fifties, with a rather cherubic face and an affable manner, and he received me not from behind a desk but at a small, round table, topped with polished, tooled leather that was decorated with sample packages of Philip Morris products. He was smoking from a pack of Parliaments. After some talk about the merchandising of cigarettes, we got around to my main question. "I think that if it were ever conclusively shown that there was some connection between smoking and, say, lung cancer, most agencies would not be advertising cigarettes," he said. "But it's easy to get stampeded, and the tobacco industry is being very much maligned. Fifty years ago, when I was a boy, my grandfather was a druggist in Alexandria, and I remember how Coca-Cola was then under the worst attack you could conceive of. People used to spread the rumor that it was a dope — the most unbelievable stories, all completely without foundation. The same thing has happened to the tobacco industry, which has been under attack for a couple of hundred years. People have been *shot*. Now the industry has been presented as a bunch of ogres trying to corrupt American youth. The fact is that I have never met a finer group in my life than the people in the tobacco industry — I'll stack them up against *any* other group for morals, ethics, and beliefs. And tobacco has given pleasure to an awful lot of people. You should not act on hunches, suspicions, and stir-ups. This cancer business, now — nobody knows about it. I have to accept that there is some connection between smoking and health, but just what it is we don't know. You can concentrate on the negative side — build a negative case for cigarettes' being banned — and ignore the positive case. Some people may be immoderate users. But I don't think any industry should be persecuted for the immoderation of its users, provided the industry hasn't promoted immoderation — and certainly the tobacco industry hasn't. You won't find anybody in the cigarette business telling you to smoke two and a half packs a day. I was having lunch the other day with a doctor, and he said, *'There's* the biggest killer in the United States! What we're doing — eating!' This anti-cigarette campaign is not a haphazard thing; it's a well-conceived, well-directed campaign from some over-all headquarters — from the timing of releases to everything else. Some of what is being put out goes so far overboard that it makes me almost sure it isn't true. They say that sixteen thousand people died last year of lung cancer. The obvious conclusion is that they were victims of cigarettes. But nothing is said about how many would die of lung cancer if all cigarette smoking stopped. If *we* pulled that trick in the advertising business, we'd be put in jail."

I remarked that I had been wondering whether Parliament's claim about Extra Margin didn't presuppose, to some degree, an element of danger to smokers.

"I have a theory that everything around us has an element of danger," Pattison said. "Your swimming pool can kill you. Cars can kill you. Coffee can kill you. Justice Holmes said that security is not the logical end of man."

At the Ted Bates advertising agency, Howard Black is one of the executives in charge of the Brown & Williamson cigarette accounts — Kool, Viceroy, Life, and a couple of other brands. In discussing his attitude toward smoking and health, he said that the position of the tobacco manufacturers was analogous to that of an automobile manufacturer confronted by statistics about automobile accidents. "I don't think that the tobacco industry would think of disbanding because one percent — or whatever the figure is — of heavy smokers died of lung cancer any more than the automobile manufacturers would think of going out of business because five hundred people get killed in auto accidents on the Fourth of July," he said. "The automobile industry is going to go on. So is the tobacco industry."

The president of Brown & Williamson is William S. Cutchins, a courteous, gray-haired southerner, who took me to lunch at the Barclay Hotel and spoke to me of his philosophy. "I went into the tobacco industry years ago, because it was a perfectly honorable business, and I set out to reap the rewards of free enterprise," he said. "I'm doing what I'm doing today because of the rewards that the free-enterprise system has to offer." He went on to say that he was as anxious as anyone else to see a well-reasoned solution to the questions that had been raised in connection with smoking and health, adding that some of the attacks on the tobacco industry were entirely unjustified, and that while many of the scientists who held "anti-cigarette views" were absolutely sincere, he did not think that the case for cigarettes had been presented to the public as it deserved to be.

I asked Cutchins what he would do if he came to accept the position that there was a connection between smoking and certain diseases.

"The first thing I'd try to do would be to correct it," he

said. "A fundamental of common decency as well as of enlightened self-interest." He advised me to read a red-covered booklet — a copy of which he had with him — called "Headline Hunting with Statistics," which was a reprint of a speech given before a group of security analysts by Robert K. Heimann, assistant to the president of the American Tobacco Company. Later, I did so. It was a full-scale attack on what the author called "the anti-cigarette crusade," and sharply questioned the statistical validity of various studies that have found a link between smoking and disease. One section of the speech wound up, "Not all of the questions are scientific ones. You might well ask whether the American Cancer Society would be spending so much time and money propagandizing anti-tobacco statistics if the millions of dollars they have solicited from the public for so many years had shed any light on the causes of cancer."

Some time later, I again encountered Heimann's name, in an article in the *Times* headlined "2 DOUBT SMOKING IS CANCER CAUSE." Here he was identified as "Dr. Robert K. Heimann, a sociologist and statistician" of the American Tobacco Company, but when I went to call on him, I saw him not in his capacity as a sociologist and statistician but in his capacity as assistant to the president of the American Tobacco Company in charge of public relations. He is a slightly built, rather poker-faced man, who was once the editor of *Forbes Magazine*. Among other things, he told me, with emphasis, that experiments using cigarette smoke had never induced lung cancer in an animal. (Dr. Hammond has said, with equal emphasis, that experimental animals have so little tolerance for cigarette smoke forced into their lungs that they do not live long enough for further investigation.)

A day or so later, Heimann arranged to have me meet his chief, Robert B. Walker, who in April of 1963 succeeded the late Paul Hahn as president of American Tobacco. In contrast to the New York headquarters of the other tobacco companies I visited – all of them very modern-looking, with lots of formica and blocks of colors – the offices of the American Tobacco Company have a certain grand, old-fashioned air, and the furniture there looks just as it must have looked in the days of the late George Washington Hill, the great tobacco-empire builder. The secretaries' filing cabinets, desks, and chairs are all made of solid oak, and on each desk is a small silver plate engraved with its occupant's name. Here and there are plaques bearing various office slogans devised by Hill, such as "Quality of Product Is Essential to Continuing Success" and "Get Your O.K. in Writing." The offices of nearly all the executives are equipped with solid-mahogany desks and chairs, and the office of the president is on an even more solid scale – a vast room, with panelled walls of bleached mahogany, chairs of mahogany and black leather, a couple of black leather sofas, and a huge desk of unbleached mahogany. When Heimann escorted me into this office, Walker, a masterful-looking, gray-haired man of fifty with a pink rose in his buttonhole, was sitting behind his great desk in what looked like a judge's chair. It was indeed a judge's chair, he told me when he got up to greet me; it had belonged to Judge Gary, the first chairman of the United States Steel Corporation.

Getting down to the purpose of my interview, Walker said, "We are facing some rough seas. But I am thoroughly convinced that the tobacco industry will survive and flourish. The people in this industry are loyal, dedicated people – people dedicated to the good of the country, people who have made a contribution to humanity. I don't want to paraphrase Winston Churchill, but I will. I don't think that any industry has given so much pleasure to so many people for so many centuries, and is so deserving of more consideration and fair play than it is now getting." Having said this, he looked across at Heimann, who was sitting on a sofa to one side of him, and remarked appraisingly, "That's pretty good. 'So much pleasure to so many people for so many centuries.' " He lit up a Lucky Strike and puffed at it with pleasure.

I said that some people felt there was a mounting weight of evidence implicating cigarettes as the source of some danger to health, and he replied, "There isn't a mounting weight of evidence. There's a mounting wave of propaganda. The hypothesis about smoking has not been proved. Now, under our American system everybody is innocent until proved guilty, and even then the verdict is subject to appeal and reappeal. This is not the case here. Many doctors subscribe to the cholesterol theory that we've all heard so much about. Cholesterol may be the killer of us all. But until it's proved, should the whole dairy industry be condemned? Should everybody give up ice cream even if it takes a few hours off your life? Some doctors say that we don't have the answers about cholesterol, and some say that we don't have the answers about tobacco. Is it fair to condemn the tobacco industry under the present circumstances? This is a seven-billion-dollar business, and the taxes on the tobacco industry last year could pay for the whole space program for a year."

Of all the tobacco-manufacturing people I talked to, Morgan J. Cramer, president of the P. Lorillard Company, which manufactures Kent and Newport cigarettes, was distinctive, for a couple of reasons. For one, he was the only executive who even mentioned (although he certainly did not elaborate on) an issue that I understood was troubling the tobacco industry – the pending lawsuits brought against individual tobacco companies by the heirs of victims of lung cancer. For another, he was the only man to concede that cigarettes might possibly contain substances worth filtering out. He didn't say that these substances were harmful, but he did say that "certain things in smoking that don't affect taste, enjoyment, or pleasure can be removed, and since there has been some question about them, they're better out than in." To that end, he said, his company had come up with a new filter that would remove phenol from the smoke. (In the available literature on smoking and health, it seems to be commonly recognized that phenol is one – but only one – of many substances in tobacco smoke that are suspected of playing a carcinogenic role.) But beyond this I found no compromise. "I don't believe that cigarettes are causing all these diseases," he said. "Cigarette smoking has been in existence a long time, and we consider that we have a serious responsibility to the smoking public. If we were convinced that cigarettes were harmful, we wouldn't be in the cigarette business."

Did he think, I asked, that cigarette companies should inform the public – by labelling or by other means – of the statistical association that is supposed to exist between smoking and disease.

"The public has been informed," he replied. "The public knows all about it."

My final interview was with Adolph J. Toigo, the president

of Lennen & Newell, the advertising agency that handles the ads and commercials for most of Lorillard's cigarette brands. Lennen & Newell annually handles about thirty million dollars' worth of Lorillard advertising. After the comparative frankness of Cramer on certain aspects of the issue of smoking and health, I hoped that Toigo might be equally informative. He is a short, gray-looking man, with graying hair, a gray mustache, and a rather pale face. He was wearing a gray suit. As we talked about the cigarette business in his big, panelled office, I found my hopes fading. "Kent has grown more than any other filter cigarette," he said. "We believe the right combination of filter and tobacco is responsible. That reflects our current campaign. Lorillard has spent a lot of money anticipating consumer requirements. There's a lot of idealism in the big corporations. I have quite an aversion to the opposite interpretation."

After a while, I asked him what he thought about the cigarette-health question.

"Well, I think it's a controversial subject on which there is no proof — no established proof — of cigarettes' being harmful," he said. "What's more, I think it's *beneficial* to smoke. Otherwise they wouldn't be doing it."

As I left Toigo's office — and the offices of Cramer, Bowling, Landry, Pattison, Black, Heimann, and Walker before him — I could have no doubt but that the lines had been drawn and the battle joined. And I could no more foresee an accommodation between the opposing forces than I could before I started.

1963

3

The Last Days of
the Cigarette Commercial
A.D. 1970

At midnight January 1st, 1971, all television and radio commercials for cigarettes go off the air for good. Their removal by that time has been required by federal law. This ban is the principal result of the Public Health Cigarette Smoking Act, which was passed by both houses of Congress in the spring of 1970 for the purpose of protecting smokers from being exposed, over public airwaves, to advertisements for a product that the Surgeon General of the United States Public Health Service has declared to be hazardous to health. The act is an extraordinary piece of legislation. It was passed in spite of massive pressure that had been brought to bear against it, and against the regulation of cigarette advertising generally, by the tobacco industry, the broadcasting industry, and their lobbyists and political allies. This was a combination that for years had proved itself invincible against a counterforce of scientists and public-health and public-interest advocates who, armed with formidable statistics on the damage to health and life caused by cigarette smoking, had sought to protect consumers by requiring all cigarette advertising to provide adequate warnings of these dangers.

The emphasis on controlling the content of cigarette advertising rather than the sale of cigarettes themselves is an indication of the power that advertising has attained in American society, particularly advertising for products that, like cigarettes, have no useful external function but that come under the merchandisers' category of "pleasure products," the need for which is essentially subjective. Such subjective needs are capable of being aroused and maintained on a socially acceptable scale with the help of advertising. Fifty years ago in this country, advertising was a mere adjunct to the selling of consumer goods; nowadays it lies at the core of the whole merchandising and consuming process.

The merchandising of cigarettes on a large scale became practical with the development, around the time of the First World War, of a slightly acid cigarette tobacco, which allowed smokers to inhale without an immediate unpleasant effect. (Tobacco smoke that is alkaline produces an automatic cough reflex when inhaled.) Mass production of cigarettes really got under way in the mid-twenties, with the help of big advertising campaigns that, in further expanding the market, employed such slogans as "Reach for a Lucky Instead of a Sweet" and "Blow Some My Way," by way of encouraging women as well as men to take up the habit. Pushed by such campaigns in the press, the per-capita consumption of cigarettes in the adult population of the United States doubled between 1920 and 1930. Between the latter half of the thirties and the latter half of the forties cigarette consumption, urged on now by hard-driving advertising campaigns on network radio as well as in the press, approximately doubled again. The increase continued in the formative period of commercial television; between 1950 and 1952, for example, the per-capita consumption of cigarettes in the adult population increased from thirty-five hundred and twenty-two cigarettes a year to thirty-eight hundred and eighty-six.

Apart from all the smoke that was being blown everybody's way, these increases in the cigarette habit had certain consequences for the adult population. The nature of these consequences showed up in a series of medical studies on the apparent effects of smoking that were conducted or completed during the fifties and the sixties. In 1950, three medical studies concluded that an ominous association existed between cigarette smoking and ill health. In 1954, the study made for the American Cancer Society by Dr. E. Cuyler Hammond, an epidemiologist, and Dr. Daniel Horn, a statistician, dwelt in great detail on the relationship between the incidence of smoking and excessive death rates. The results of the study made the front pages of the press in this country but were virtually ignored on network-television news shows — which, as it happened, were nearly all sponsored by cigarette companies.

In 1957, a further study by Drs. Hammond and Horn elaborated upon these conclusions. In 1962, a report of a committee of the Royal College of Physicians in Great Britain declared, "Cigarette smoking is a cause of lung cancer and bronchitis, and probably contributes to the development of coronary heart disease and various other less common diseases." In January, 1964, a report issued by a select advisory committee to the Surgeon General concluded that cigarette smoking is causally related to lung cancer in males. It found an association between the incidence of cigarette smoking and that of heart disease, and it found the habit to be the most important of the causes of chronic bronchitis and to increase the risk of dying from emphysema. In summary, the Surgeon General's report found that "cigarette smoking is a health hazard of sufficient importance in the United States to warrant appropriate remedial action."

This call for remedial action aroused officials of the normally passive Federal Trade Commission. In June, 1964, Paul Rand Dixon, the chairman of the Commission, declared in testimony before the House Committee on Interstate and Foreign Commerce that the F.T.C. had decided on a ruling that a strong health warning be put on all cigarette packages and appear in all cigarette advertising, including advertising on television. The committee gave Mr. Dixon a hostile reception. The F.T.C.'s proposed ruling led those sympathetic to the tobacco industry to accuse it of discriminating against a legally sold product and of usurping the legislative functions of Congress. The F.T.C. got no support from President Johnson, either; in fact, the White House is said to have intervened to get the agency to delay putting its ruling into effect. All told, no matter what the Surgeon General said about the malign effects of cigarette smoking, the opposition to the regulation of cigarette advertising was of formidable proportions. Tobacco is a one-billion-dollar-a-year agricultural product, a crop that the Department of Agriculture regularly subsidizes with millions of dollars in price supports. It is a ten-billion-dollar-a-year consumer product, from which federal and state governments derive almost four billion dollars a year in tax revenues, and tobacco advertising has accounted for about eight percent of the entire advertising revenues of the television networks. At the time of the Surgeon General's report, the tobacco companies were spending two hundred and fifty million dollars a year on advertising, three-fifths of which went for TV commercials. The weight of the combined forces of the tobacco industry and its allies was soon felt in the form of proposed legislation called the Cigarette Labelling and Advertising Bill of 1965, which purported to protect smokers by making a warning on cigarette packages ("Caution: Cigarette Smoking May Be Hazardous to Your Health") mandatory but would actually constitute a legislative triumph for the tobacco lobby, in that it prohibited the F.T.C. or any other federal agency from requiring tobacco companies to include a health warning in their cigarette advertising for the next four years. The tobacco industry then went on merchandising cigarettes with renewed vigor.

Over the years, television had given the tobacco companies a remarkable tool for persuading people to smoke particular brands of cigarettes, because television advertising showed what print and radio advertising couldn't — smoking in action. It showed young people puffing away, inhaling deeply and blowing smoke around with obvious pleasure, and always in settings that made the habit seem attractive. The habituating nature of cigarettes made appeals of this kind increasingly effective as television became the overwhelmingly predomi-

nant form of mass communication in this country. For a
month or two after the 1964 Surgeon General's report, the
sales of cigarettes in the United States showed a significant
drop, but sales gradually recovered and rose above their
previous level. While the tobacco industry was vehemently
denying that there was any causal connection between
smoking and disease, individual cigarette companies reacted
to the unwelcome suggestion by introducing and advertising
new brands of filter cigarettes, which, the television advertising for them implied without actually talking about health,
were somehow a lot more beneficial, or somehow less harmful, to smokers than unfiltered cigarettes.

In a short time, with relentless advertising and promotion,
the consumption of filter cigarettes soared. In 1950, when
commercial television was just beginning, eighty-three percent of the cigarette market was given over to five brands —
Camel, Lucky Strike, Chesterfield, Philip Morris, and Pall
Mall. But in the fifties, with the introduction of Kent and its
"Micronite Filter," of Winston, which was alleged to taste
good "like a cigarette should," and of the new Marlboro,
featuring the clean outdoors and the Marlboro Man in the
cowboy hat, the filter brands quickly began taking over. One
of the striking features of the mass marketing of a great
number of consumer products in the past twenty years is the
increasing blandness of the taste that has been built into
these products. This change has applied to everything from
beer to bread, and it is not surprising, given the disquieting
news about the relationship between smoking and health,
that this principle should be made to apply to cigarettes, too.
Today, the difference in taste between one brand of filter
cigarettes and another in a particular class — regular or

menthol, for example – may be hardly detectable to a smoker wearing a blindfold. But the packaging, the appearance, and other aspects of the "brand imaging" are something else. As these merchandisers are fond of saying, no other object that people carry around is more often handled except money. And the close contact a smoker maintains with his cigarettes – a pack-a-day smoker reaches for the pack twenty times a day, picks up a cigarette when he's tense, habitually handles and puffs at it while he's making the decisions that his working day calls for, and continues puffing away hour upon hour in his free time – makes the cigarette he uses enough a part of his living style so that distinctive packaging and appearance provide a marked identity to the particular brands a merchandiser is promoting aside from its actual taste. A brand manager at one of the big tobacco companies told me recently, not without pride, "What we're selling is illusion." In the age of commercial television, the number of major brands of cigarettes on the market has grown from half a dozen to almost thirty, in all shapes and sizes; by 1968, filter cigarettes, which at the beginning of commercial television had accounted for one and a half percent of the cigarette market, accounted for perhaps seventy-five percent. The wild proliferation of filter brands continually elevated the advertising revenues of the television networks, because the cost of introducing a new brand went into millions of dollars. And the tobacco companies kept increasing their promotional efforts on TV, because the capture of even a tiny part of the market meant high profits. The battle of the filters was fought on the television screens across the country with round-ups, people running around in green fields or sailing on green seas, and with fusillades of jingles. If the problems of lung cancer and emphysema among smokers could be solved by song, the television commercials the tobacco industry put out would have eliminated those illnesses in a week.

In the latter part of the sixties, the big new development in cigarette advertising was the hundred-millimetre cigarette, the promotion of which was led by the campaign for Benson & Hedges 100's, which Philip Morris had been putting out as a minor brand in regular size. The advertising agency chosen for this campaign was the relatively new firm of Wells, Rich, Greene, headed by Mary Wells Lawrence, who is one of the most skillful advertisers around. Through a series of gag-filled commercials in which smokers of the new brand suffered mishaps because of the unusual length of the cigarette — getting the cigarette caught in a closing elevator door or burning a hole in the smoker's newspaper — the Wells, Rich, Greene campaign made an instant impression on the cigarette market. What Mrs. Lawrence believed, she told me when the campaign was under way, was that in the new longer cigarette "we had an elegant, classy product, tied in with affluence, appealing to mass buyers between twenty and forty who are slightly higher in education than most, and more sophisticated - people who've seen their supermarkets turn into the Folies-Bergères, people who are used to being entertained, people who are winner-oriented." One of the things that lay behind the Wells, Rich, Greene campaign was an approach in which the advertiser attempted to come to a kind of implicit understanding with the viewer that most advertising was, yes, rather a nuisance, and that in return for deciding to buy Benson & Hedges 100's the viewer would be spared a hard sell for the brand over the tube. It was an appeal to a certain kind of "knowing" viewer. It was also an appeal that made smoking seem a laughing matter – another plus for the industry. The result of the campaign was that sales of Benson & Hedges 100's rose from one billion six hundred million cigarettes in 1966 to fourteen billion four hundred million cigarettes in 1970, for a total sale of well over fifty billion cigarettes in the four-year period.

Then, there were the commercials for Silva Thins, a hundred-millimetre cigarette that was introduced by the American Tobacco Company. The Silva Thins commercials seemed to have been designed for the sado-masochistic crowd as well as the hundred-millimetre crowd. They featured a male model with dark wraparound glasses and a surly expression who, in successive commercials, wordlessly show-ed by boorish or brutal treatment of beautiful girls that he preferred Silva Thins to their company. Driving along a deserted highway, he would reject the attempts that a pretty girl riding with him made to talk with him. He would knock her arm aside as she offered him a light. And when the girl picked up his pack of Silva Thins, he would jam the brakes on, fling open the door on the girl's side, brusquely order the girl out, then drive off, change his mind, back up, and, instead of picking the girl up again, grab from her hand the pack of Silva Thins and screech off, leaving her stranded by the roadside. The Silva Thins man would also leave girls stranded in elevators, in motorbike sidecars in Paris, in gon-dolas in Venice, and even in cable cars in the Alps. "Ciga-rettes are like girls. The best ones are thin and rich," a Silva Thins announcer intoned in a later series of commercials. The slogan with which the American Tobacco people accom-panied the stranded-girl commercials was "Silva Thins, the

Impossible Cigarette" — impossible, presumably, because the cigarette was "lowest in tar and nicotine of all 100's . . . yet Silva Thins taste better." Such television campaigns sold more than four and a half billion Silva Thins in 1970.

And there was the TV advertising campaign for Virginia Slims, a hundred-millimetre cigarette introduced by Philip Morris shortly after Silva Thins came on the market. The Virginia Slims commercials began with a scene showing, in archly slapstick fashion, the lowly role of women in an earlier era: "In 1915, Mrs. Cynthia Robinson was caught smoking in the cellar behind the preserves. Although she was thirty-four, her husband sent her straight to her room." They ended with a shot of a swinging, almost aggressively self-confident girl — the kind of girl likely to give a hard time to any character in wraparound glasses who might try to throw her out of his car — who was smoking a Virginia Slim and was obviously enjoying the experience. The message of the Virginia Slims commercials, sung to a strong brassy-contemporary beat, was "You've come a long way, baby, to get where you've got to today. You've got your own cigarette now, baby. You've come a long, long way." Within a year of the opening of this campaign of liberation, the sale of Virginia Slims rose to four and a half billion cigarettes, or two hundred and twenty-five million packs. And by the time cigarette commercials went off the air for good, Virginia Slims was selling at the annual rate of nearly five and a half billion cigarettes; that is, more than one hundred million packs. One of the considerations underlying the highly successful campaign for Virginia Slims, and the very large sales of other brands in the same period, was that over the years the number of women smokers had been increasing steadily and had come to constitute a large share — about forty percent — of the total cigarette market.

Women had also come a long, long way in other respects connected with smoking. Between 1930 and 1967, the proportion of women in the adult population who were smokers rose from ten percent to an estimated thirty-five percent. And in that same period the rate of lung cancer among women increased approximately fourfold. According to officials of the American Cancer Society, forty-five percent of the women who died of lung cancer in the nineteen-fifties and sixties were regular cigarette smokers.

The television campaigns persuading people to smoke cigarettes went on relentlessly through the fifties and sixties, too. In the mid-sixties, while interviewing people in the tobacco business and the cigarette-advertising business on their attitudes toward smoking and health, I did not come across a single executive who gave any credence to the Surgeon General's report. Thus: Did the moving force behind the Benson & Hedges campaign that began in 1966 – Mary Wells Lawrence herself – believe there was any causal relationship between smoking and lung cancer or other diseases? "My business is the advertising business," Mrs. Lawrence told me. "I am not a scientist. The information provided to me on this subject – and that includes the Surgeon General's report – leaves me in a state of total indecisiveness. When the government shows me beyond doubt that no matter who you are and what your makeup is cigarettes can cause you to contract these diseases, I'll search my soul about the moral problem." She added, "I sell liquors, automobiles, airline travel, and cosmetics – life has all sorts of opportunities. It is impossible for me to be running an advertising agency and to make up my mind to advertise one legally sold product and not another."

As the promotional gimmicks, the sprightly gags, the

jingles, and the laughter in the cigarette commercials increased, so did the mass of evidence on the association between cigarette smoking and health. In 1967, a review by the Public Health Service of current scientific studies on the subject since the Surgeon General's report pointed further toward the causal nature of the relationship between smoking, certain diseases, and premature death. The report found, "Cigarette smokers have substantially higher rates of death and disability than their non-smoking counterparts in the population," and said, "Cigarette smokers tend to die at earlier ages and experience more days of disability than comparable non-smokers." It noted, further, that a substantial portion of these early deaths and disabilities would not have occurred if those affected had not smoked, and that "if it were not for cigarette smoking, practically none of the earlier deaths from lung cancer would have occurred." The response of the cigarette industry to these findings was to put into that year's cigarette commercials and sponsored programs on television about two hundred and seventeen million dollars, or approximately twenty-three million dollars more than it had put into them the previous year.

Before long, however, the tobacco industry and the broadcasting industry were in for a bit of a shock. In June, 1967, the Federal Communications Commission ruled that its "fairness doctrine" — which provided that when allegations concerning controversial subjects of public importance are made on the air broadcasters must provide air time, on request, for citizens who dispute these allegations and wish to make their own views known — applied to the advertising of cigarettes on the air. The ruling was the result of representations made to the F.C.C. by a young New York lawyer named John F. Banzhaf III, and it threw the tobacco and broadcasting industries into considerable turmoil and confusion, for it led to an obligatory granting of millions of dollars' worth of air time each year for the televising of anti-smoking commercials.

A while ago, Banzhaf described for me the genesis and some of the consequences of this unprecedented ruling by the F.C.C. "I went into this strictly as a personal project," he told me at his office at George Washington University, in Washington, D.C., where he is now an associate professor of law. "I don't want to paint a picture of myself as some kind of anti-smoking fanatic, although it so happens that I've never smoked. I began to think of the project out of a concern not so much about the dangers of smoking as about the tactics being used in advertising cigarettes. I was concerned about the use of the public airwaves to seduce young people into taking up smoking without any attempt to tell the other side of the story on television and radio. I felt that I might be able to redress the balance, even with my own very limited resources, through taking advantage of the fairness doctrine of the F.C.C. It looked as though the fairness doctrine offered a legal loophole that might allow me a large output for a small amount of input." Banzhaf has done legal work on computer-technology cases, and he sometimes uses the vocabulary of computer technicians. "I couldn't take on the networks directly," Banzhaf went on. "The F.C.C. doesn't license networks – only individual stations – and the Commission requires that when you are requesting time on the air you have to take up the request with individual stations before approaching the F.C.C. So instead of tackling one of the networks, I wrote to the management of WCBS-TV, in New York, and asked that free time be made available to present the other side of the story from that being given in cigarette commercials. This request was denied, as I expected. My next step was to file a petition with the F.C.C. in which, having presented the facts of the request I'd made to WCBS-TV and the refusal I had met with, I asked the F.C.C. to rule that, given the Surgeon General's report and other scientific reports on the relationship between smoking and health, cigarette smoking was a controversial issue of public importance, and that it was therefore proper for the Commission to order radio and TV stations to provide reply time for the presentation of views on the dangers of smoking."

Banzhaf presented his petition to the F.C.C. early in January, 1967, and after mulling it over for some time the Commission, on Friday, June 2, 1967, ruled that its fairness doctrine did indeed apply to cigarette advertising on radio and television, and that broadcasters carrying cigarette commercials were under an obligation to provide "a significant amount of time" to citizens who wished to point out that smoking "may be hazardous to the smoker's health." Banzhaf had requested that the rebuttal time provided for anti-smoking information on the air be "roughly proportionate" to the entire amount of time being devoted to cigarette advertising on the air. In its decision, the F.C.C. appears to have interpreted this request as one for equal time, and this it specifically ruled out. However, Henry Geller, then chief counsel for the Commission, gave his informal opinion, in a subsequent press interview, that a ratio of one anti-smoking message to three cigarette commercials seemed to him to correspond reasonably to the "significant" amount of time the Commission had in mind.

The Monday morning after Banzhaf learned of the F.C.C. decision, he was called in, he says, to the office of the head of the law firm where he worked. "I found out that one of our firm's clients was one of the Big Six tobacco manufacturers," he says. "Obviously, it was an awkward situation from a professional point of view. I went off to think things over, and my tentative conclusion was that, having accomplished what I had in making cigarette commercials subject to the fairness doctrine, I might as well bow out and allow some of the major private health organizations to carry the ball from there on. I'd put a great deal of effort into preparing the petition to the F.C.C.; the job I had was the first I'd held with a law firm; my personal financial resources were very limited, to say the least; and I knew that the F.C.C. decision was just the beginning of a long fight, because it was certain to be attacked by the tobacco industry and the broadcasting industry in protracted legal proceedings, and undertaking the defense of the decision that was certainly going to be necessary seemed obviously beyond my capacity at the time."

Banzhaf further suspected — and his suspicion came to be fully realized — that a sizable obstacle that would have to be overcome if the application of the F.C.C. fairness doctrine to cigarette advertising should eventually be upheld in the courts was the problem of insuring that television stations would make serious efforts to comply with the F.C.C. decision. One of the basic requirements for enforcement of the decision would be to have monitorings made of the time given over to cigarette commercials and anti-smoking mes-

sages by stations throughout the country. Most citizens might
assume that an agency with such far-flung responsibilities as
the F.C.C. – the issuing and renewing of public and private
broadcasting licenses and the complex regulation of virtually
every civilian use of the public airwaves, from the smallest
citizens'-band walkie-talkie to the largest television station –
would necessarily have a large and efficient monitoring
service to insure that its regulations were being complied
with. The fact is, however, that the F.C.C. possesses a total
permanent investigative staff of four people to check up on
possible violations of its rules concerning broadcast content
as it is officially considered to affect the public interest –
and then only on the basis of complaints. As far as Banzhaf
was concerned, that meant relying on four government men
to keep track of violations of the F.C.C. fairness doctrine as
it affected the nearly one thousand television stations and
nearly seven thousand radio stations. It meant, in fact, that
such F.C.C. program-monitoring operations hardly existed.
Of course, the F.C.C. could easily have used its authority
under the Communications Act of 1934 to require stations to
make formal periodic reports on the number of cigarette
commercials and anti-smoking commercials they were running. But the Commission did not request such reports.

Since the F.C.C. clearly didn't have the means of keeping
track of the effect of its own decisions upon the industry it
was supposed to be regulating, and since Banzhaf himself
didn't, either, he thought that the most practical way to get
some monitoring of the broadcasters' degree of compliance
with the F.C.C. ruling would be to have it undertaken by
private citizens who were active members of health organizations such as the American Cancer Society. Accordingly, he

told me, he wrote letters to these organizations and to the National Interagency Council on Smoking and Health – an organization that carries out some coördinating functions between the public-information arms of the American Cancer Society, the National Tuberculosis Association, the American Heart Association, and other health societies – and outlined the steps needed to sustain the F.C.C. decision.

"After I'd sent off the letters, I was invited to a meeting of this Interagency Council, and when I turned up at it I pointed out to the representatives of these health organizations that the first petition opposing the F.C.C. decision had already been filed with the F.C.C. – I forget whom it was on behalf of – and that within sixty days someone had to answer that petition with sound legal arguments if the F.C.C. decision was to be upheld," Banzhaf said. "I felt very strongly that the decision could not be saved unless responsible health organizations banded together to support it with competent legal counsel. But the representatives of the health organizations I was trying to persuade turned me down, one after another. In words I'll never forget. One of them said to me, 'Let me tell you the economic facts of life. My organization depends on free broadcasting time for our fund-raising drives. We are not going to jeopardize that time by getting involved in this move.' Another told me, 'We're a health organization, not a legal organization. We can't get involved in legal action.'

"Others suggested that they felt they could get more from the broadcasters by coöperating with them in a friendly way than by becoming their legal antagonists. Even before the F.C.C. decision, the American Cancer Society had been preparing some cautionary commercials about smoking. Its representatives felt they could have these spots used on the air here and there, and didn't want to injure their chances of doing that. Also, the health organizations were used to thinking of the problem just in terms of disease. Their attitude was that you don't *sue* a disease. They were all very sympathetic, but they felt themselves dependent on the good will of the broadcasters, so they simply weren't prepared to get into a fight. In sum, they wouldn't do anything and wanted to leave it to me to act. I felt rather bitter about this.

"All that summer of 1967, petitions to the F.C.C. to rescind its decision were being filed. All together, there were about a dozen of them. The petitions filed included those on behalf of the three major networks, of the National Association of Broadcasters, of well over a hundred individual TV and radio stations, of the six major tobacco companies in this country, of the Tobacco Institute, and even of the Federal Communications Bar Association, a group of attorneys practicing in the communications industry. The petitions were filed by some of the top law firms in the country, including the Washington firms of Arnold & Porter — the firm Abe Fortas left to go on the Supreme Court — and Covington & Burling.

"With great difficulty, I decided to go ahead myself and to prepare arguments for presentation to the F.C.C. in support of my original petition and against the legal arguments opposing it and the F.C.C.'s decision. I was continuing with my job at the law firm, but felt uncertain about my position there, and the time I had available for this outside private project was very limited. But I got my reply brief supporting the original decision in, and I remember that on September 8th, a Friday, I left my office at eleven-thirty at night. I picked up an early edition of Saturday's *New York Times* and read that the F.C.C. had rejected the broadcasters' and tobacco industry's petitions and had unanimously reaffirmed its decision requiring a significant amount of free rebuttal time to be offered against cigarette commercials. When I read that, I went right back to my office and got to work again. The reason for that was my knowledge that the reaffirmation of the F.C.C.'s decision could now be reviewed in any of the federal courts of appeal in the country, and that petitions for review would certainly be presented to those courts. I knew I'd have to be prepared for real trouble."

The trouble that Banzhaf had in mind was the possibility that the tobacco and broadcasting forces, in petitioning the federal courts of appeal to review the F.C.C. decision, might take advantage of Banzhaf's limited resources by deliberately filing a petition in a court difficult for Banzhaf to get to from New York – a court in Los Angeles, for example. Also, he reasoned, they might file a petition for review in a court they thought would be friendly to their cause – a covert but widespread practice known in the legal profession as "forum shopping." Banzhaf quickly decided that the best way to forestall such moves was to do his own forum shopping. From his point of view, the most convenient forum for consideration of the issue was in Washington – the federal Court of Appeals for the District of Columbia Circuit. Three months earlier, that court had upheld the Constitutionality of the fairness doctrine in vigorous terms. However, he couldn't pick his court as easily as all that, because the choice of the particular court to review a petition is determined by where the petition for review is first filed. Furthermore, in the normal course of events a petitioner before a court has to have *lost* a cause – not won it, as Banzhaf had – in order to present a petition for review. Accordingly, Banzhaf worked very late that night preparing a court petition *against* the F.C.C.'s reaffirmation of its decision to require air time for anti-smoking messages. The ground he chose for his petition for review was that the Commission had denied what it had interpreted as his original demand for equal time for rebuttal of cigarette commercials and had granted only "a significant amount of time." Having prepared this petition, he flew to Washington the next morning, rushed downtown, and filed the petition with a clerk of the U.S. Court of Appeals, who, fortunately for Banzhaf, happened to be there although it was Saturday. Thus Banzhaf established — or so he hoped — a forum that would prevent lawyers representing the tobacco and broadcasting interests from facing him in court territory they might consider most favorable to their side.

Two days after Banzhaf filed his petition for review, an assembly known as the World Conference on Smoking and Health, which was sponsored by the National Interagency Council on Smoking and Health and was managed by the American Cancer Society, began a series of meetings at the Waldorf-Astoria. The purpose of the conference was to receive and discuss new medical and scientific findings on the connection between cigarette smoking and ill health, and to discuss public and private programs for educating and warning people about the hazards of smoking. One of the introductory speakers at the conference was Senator Robert F. Kennedy, and Banzhaf says that as a result of a talk he had with one of the Senator's assistants just before the health conference convened, Senator Kennedy incorporated into his speech a recommendation that the health organizations help provide legal assistance for the defense of the F.C.C.'s decision. On the third day of the conference, Banzhaf himself spoke before one of its committees and urged such assistance. The committee made a similar recommendation, but, according to Banzhaf, the major health organizations reconsidered their position and again declined to use their funds to engage in litigation on cigarettes. The same day that Banzhaf made his appeal to the conference, the National Association of Broadcasters, in association with one of its member stations, filed its own petition for review of the F.C.C. decision.

"They filed with the Court of Appeals in Richmond, Virginia — which, of course, is deep in the heart of Tobaccoland," Banzhaf told me. "The broadcasters, having filed their petition in Richmond, then came back to the Court of Appeals in Washington and filed a twenty-page motion citing twenty or thirty cases and claiming that my petition in Washington was defective and should be dismissed — the idea being to change the scene from Washington to Richmond. Under court rules, I had five days to reply to the broadcasters' motion. It wasn't much time for me, and normally it's common custom for one party in proceedings of this sort to permit an extension to the opposite side to give it reasonable time to prepare its arguments. I telephoned my opponents and asked if, in view of the fact that I had a full-time job, they'd grant me a reasonable extension of time. But the other side said no. It was the old technique of overwhelming your opponent, blitzing him with papers. I just had to work a little harder. In five days, I prepared a forty-page answer to their twenty-page motion, and the eventual result of these filings was that the court upheld my position to the extent that the case stayed in the Court of Appeals in Washington."

People in Washington who are familiar with the background of the F.C.C. decision and the appellate-court proceedings in which the decision was upheld find Banzhaf's act in originally demanding air time for cautionary messages about cigarette smoking a most resourceful way of publicizing its hazards at minimum cost, and for that, they believe, he deserves great credit. However, their admiration for his resourcefulness is tempered by reservations concerning what they think is his occasional propensity for personal publicity, in contrast to the manner of other and more self-effacing people whose contributions over the years to the cause of informing the public of the relationship betwen smoking and health were at least as fundamental. And, indeed, to talk with Banzhaf at any length about public awareness of the relationship between cigarette smoking and health, one would hardly think that such prime movers in the field as Drs. Hammond and Horn, whose study in 1954 first brought the issue to wide public attention, and Dr. Luther Terry, the Surgeon General of the United States between 1961 and 1965, had ever existed. Although Banzhaf's disappointment at being unable to get financial help from national health organizations is understandable, there are a few matters that his account of his relations with the health organizations ignores. These have been dwelt upon by Clifton R. Read, an official of the American Cancer Society, in an interview.

"At the Cancer Society, we had mixed feelings about entering the legal action in defense of the F.C.C. decision ordering free rebuttal time to cigarette commercials on the air," Read told me. "We were very much pleased at what Banzhaf had originally accomplished, and when he urged us to provide financial assistance for the defense of the decision we asked our own counsel to explore the situation. A member of his firm talked in Washington with counsel for the F.C.C., and he reported to us that the Commission felt that the principal burden of defending the F.C.C. decision would fall upon the Commission, and that the Commission did not feel that it needed any help from us in defending its decision. Our lawyer agreed. He told us that in his opinion the F.C.C. had a very strong case and had the help of excellent attorneys, and that he thought it would win in the courts without any help from us."

Unlike the American Cancer Society, the National Tuberculosis Association decided to submit an *amicus-curiae* brief in support of the F.C.C. decision. But although Banzhaf went before the Court of Appeals and argued in the proceedings he had started, the principal burden of defending the F.C.C. decision in court, as the Cancer Society people had expected, fell upon counsel for the F.C.C. itself, and the F.C.C.'s success was clear-cut. The court held that, "as a public-health measure addressed to a unique danger authenticated by official and congressional action," the F.C.C. ruling on significant time for rebuttal of cigarette commercials constituted proper protection of the public interest under the provisions of the Communications Act.

Whatever the necessity of Banzhaf's intervention in the court proceedings, there is little doubt that the next actions he took on the anti-smoking front were the cause of a lot of coughing and choking in the broadcasting and tobacco industries. Convinced that he was going to get only limited coöperation in his fight from the big, established health organizations, he decided to leave the law firm he had been working for and set up an organization of his own, in which he could devote full time to the problem of broadcast cigarette advertising. The idea of forming his own organization grew out of an article he had read in the *Times* about the Environmental Defense Fund, a coalition of lawyers and scientists that had been formed for the purpose of pursuing litigation that conservation groups like the National Audubon Society were reluctant to engage in directly. The Environmental Defense Fund is financed by foundations and contributions from the public. With this as a cue, Banzhaf formed an organization called Action on Smoking and Health (ASH) to pursue legal action on behalf of education about smoking, and established headquarters in a tiny temporary office near the United Nations. ASH was, and still is, a very small outfit, financed by public appeals.

"I knew that the broadcasters were not going to comply properly with the F.C.C. decision unless they had to," Banzhaf told me some time ago. "They were beginning to run anti-smoking commercials that were being prepared and distributed to stations by various health groups like the Cancer Society, but they weren't showing nearly enough of them. I felt that what I had to do was create a fear among the broadcasters that I could do something to them if they didn't comply fully. I had to monitor the stations to determine their degree of compliance, but, of course, the monitoring I could do was limited. I decided that the best thing was to monitor the output of a large station to determine how much free time it was giving for the rebuttal of cigarette commercials, and if it wasn't giving adequate time I needed to file a detailed complaint on its violations of the F.C.C. rule with the Commission, so that no station in the country could be sure I wouldn't file against it. So I chose to monitor

WNBC-TV. I monitored its programming in prime time for approximately two weeks, with the help of friends, and then in March, 1968, I filed a petition with the F.C.C. asking the Commission to revoke WNBC-TV's license in the middle of its current term. Our petition said our monitoring showed that the ratio of smoking commercials to anti-smoking commercials in prime time on WNBC-TV was ten to one instead of the three to one the Commission found reasonable. We asked for revocation of the station's license on the ground that the station was violating F.C.C. regulations − specifically, refusing to implement the fairness doctrine − and thus violating the terms of its franchise to operate in the public interest. At that time, I might remark, the F.C.C. hadn't done anything remotely like revoking a major television station's license. The Commission was happily rubber-stamping license renewals as they came due.

"I knew, of course, that we had only a thousand-to-one chance of getting WNBC-TV's license revoked. But I also knew that the value of the station was something like a hundred million dollars. That doesn't even include studios and transmitters − that's the probable market worth of the frequency that the government allows the owners to operate on, free of charge. We thought we would give the station something to be afraid of when we presented our petition. Who wants to take even a one-in-a-thousand chance of losing a hundred million dollars?

"WNBC-TV challenged our petition. Their people claimed that the ratio we had given of ten cigarette commercials to one anti-smoking message was inaccurate. It was close to three or four to one, they said. But we challenged *their* challenge, and asked them to document their claim. We found that when the station had run two commercials, one right after the other, for two different brands of cigarettes that just happened to be manufactured by the same company it was counting them as *one* commercial, and also that it was claiming that its so-called billboard announcements for cigarettes — 'This program is brought to you by Marlboro' — weren't commercials at all. We demanded and got the schedule for the anti-smoking messages it was carrying, and when we checked it we found out that while all the cigarette commercials it was running were being carried in prime time, a substantial number of the anti-smoking messages weren't — they were being broadcast at times like 2:30 A.M. or 6:38 A.M. WNBC-TV's explanation for running anti-smoking spots at 6:38 A.M. was that it wanted to reach children with them before they left for school."

As a result of Banzhaf's petition, the F.C.C., though it denied the demand for a revocation of the station's license, ruled that the station would have to run a greater ratio of anti-smoking messages to cigarette commercials than the current one, and run more of the messages in prime air time. This ruling concerning anti-smoking messages had the effect that Banzhaf had anticipated: the management of other television stations around the country began to be less laggard in complying with the F.C.C.'s fairness doctrine as it applied to anti-smoking messages. Through ASH, Banzhaf has tried to keep them alert by legal sniping tactics here and there. Thus, he has recalled, when a chain of stations in Indiana broadcast an editorial opposing a recommendation by the Federal Trade Commission that cigarette commercials be banned from the air, ASH asked the stations for free time to reply. The management of the stations refused the request, whereupon Banzhaf filed a complaint with the F.C.C. asking for revocation of the stations' licenses on the ground that the station owners had refused to comply with the F.C.C.'s fairness doctrine. "All that we were asking for was three or four minutes of air time, yet, upon our complaint, the owners filed a response that weighed in at over two pounds," Banzhaf said. As a result of Banzhaf's complaint, the F.C.C. ruled that the stations involved must provide free air time for a reply to the editorial on the smoking-and-advertising issue.

The American Cancer Society people appear to have done no substantial amount of direct monitoring of the time given to anti-smoking messages on individual television stations during this period. Read, of the Cancer Society, feels that, except for the first six months following the F.C.C.'s ruling on the fairness doctrine as it applied to cigarette commercials, the networks have complied with the F.C.C. ruling to a "reasonable" extent. However, he concedes that Banzhaf's aggressive tactics of bombarding stations and the F.C.C. with complaints and petitions may well have helped remind station owners of their obligation to comply.

The effect of all this upon the activities of the tobacco companies on the airwaves was highly noticeable. In addition to seeing the endless cigarette commercials showing smiling young couples running carefree in rolling countryside and prancing along ocean beaches to indicate the benign qualities of the cigarettes they were puffing away at, viewers now also began to see, sandwiched between segments of programs, a closeup shot of a serious-faced man who would hold up a cigarette and soberly ask, "Have you ever thought what happens when you smoke a cigarette?" After a pause, he would add, grimly, "*We* have," whereupon the words "American Cancer Society" would flash on the screen and the message would be over. It took only ten seconds, but its effect on the television viewer who happened to have a cigarette in his mouth as he watched it tended to be disconcerting.

Besides being caught in mid-puff by this particular message, the home audience became exposed to a number of longer anti-smoking messages, which seemed to have the capacity of acting upon the existing crowd of cigarette commercials like antibodies grappling with some bacterial swarm. Against the commercials that displayed young people examining the filters on their cigarettes with approval, viewers saw an anti-smoking message that opened with a shot of a cigarette lying flat, pointed toward the viewer. Suddenly the cigarette would come to life, coil up like a snake, ominously rattle its filter-tip tail, and strike with its lighted end right toward the viewer, while an announcer's voice asked, "What does a cigarette have to *do* to you before you get our message?" and "American Cancer Society" flashed on the screen again. Another message showed, in rapid succession, a series of warning signals – red traffic lights, a "Flammable" sign, a "Poison" label, and finally a warning label on a cigarette package. "We receive many warnings in our life," a narrator declared. "And sometimes they can save our life." The voice continued, against the sound of a cough, "This message is brought to you by the American Cancer Society."

Some of the most effective of these anti-smoking commercials were turned out by the New York advertising agency of Lord, Geller, Federico & Partners, which produced them at cost – and with producers and directors donating their time – for the American Cancer Society. One of them, which seems to have been designed to deal with the Marlboro Man theme, showed a confrontation at a saloon bar between some unshaven characters wearing ten-gallon hats. The script ran as follows:

> Various shots of bad guy's accomplices smoking as they watch good guy standing at bar.
> MLS [medium long shot] of bad guy as he walks through door of saloon with cigarette dangling from mouth.
> Good guy, standing at bar, turns noticing bad guy walking through the door.
> BAD GUY: We figured (*cough*) you'd (*cough*) be here.
> Bad guy and accomplices begin coughing uncontrollably, unable to shoot at good guy. Good guy, disgusted by the coughing, knocks bad guy aside and leaves the saloon.

Upon which, the word "Cancer" zoomed up on the screen and a voice-over announcer said, "Cigarettes - they're killers."

Richard J. Lord, who is president of Lord, Geller, Federico, had considerable familiarity with the style of cigarette commercials, having been at one time a cigarette-commercial copywriter at the Young & Rubicam agency and at another time a "creative supervisor" on cigarette accounts at the Benton & Bowles agency. At Young & Rubicam, in the late fifties, Lord was a leading member of a group assigned to promote Kent cigarettes and their Micronite Filter, under the slogan "Kent Is the Answer." On another front at Y. & R., he promoted Newport cigarettes, devised for them the slogan "A Hint of Mint," and wrote a lot of commercials showing young couples frolicking and smoking in bucolic surroundings — precisely the note that another of his Cancer Society anti-smoking messages took aim at. Then, at Benton & Bowles, in the early sixties, he wrote part of a series of commercials for Parliament cigarettes, featuring the Parliament "recessed filter, a clean quarter-inch away" — a device that was claimed to give the smoker "extra margin."

Lord told me that when his own advertising agency was making the anti-smoking messages it encountered some difficulty in finding actors to play the parts. "It was hard to get actors for this sort of thing because they were afraid they might have to give up the lucrative fees and residuals that the tobacco companies pay for parts in cigarette commercials," he said. "The Cancer Society paid a flat buy-out to actors, without residuals for replays, and it came to only three hundred and twenty dollars, whereas, say, a nationally run Winston or Salem commercial could be a little annuity for an actor for a couple of years. The average income from residuals is probably something like five thousand dollars for a year or more, but if the actor hits with a commercial that is *really* widely replayed, he could make between ten thousand and fifteen thousand dollars a year out of it. That's a lot for a hungry actor. Some actors were afraid that even if they didn't happen to be the type for cigarette commercials they might be blackballed by agencies that *did* cigarette commercials. Well, for this particular anti-smoking message [one parodying the happiness shown in cigarette commercials] we had to hunt around quite a bit to collect a cast. We must have seen forty or fifty people. We'd have actors signed up and then find them backing away. We had one guy signed up for a shooting call at 8 A.M., and at five thirty the evening before we got a call from his agent, who said he wouldn't let the actor play the part. We pointed out that the guy couldn't lose parts in cigarette commercials by appearing in an anti-smoking spot, because he didn't even smoke. The agent said,

'I'm going to *teach* him to smoke, if that will get him in a cigarette commercial.' Eventually, we came up with a few people who believed in what we were doing. Most of them were nonprofessionals. One of them was a waitress at a restaurant on Eighty-sixth Street who looked just like the sort of girl who might appear in a cigarette commercial. They were all great, and really worked hard. To get the rights to play 'Smoke Gets in Your Eyes,' we went to Chappell & Co., the music publishers who own the Kern copyright. Representatives of a cigarette company had been there before us. They'd tried to buy the song for one of their brands. But Chappell & Co. had turned them down. We explained what we wanted. The man we talked to at Chappell happened to have just given up smoking. We got the rights to play 'Smoke Gets in Your Eyes' in a Cancer Society anti-smoking message for just a hundred and sixty-eight dollars and fifty cents, which represented the bare cost of the legal paperwork involved. The messages have been a pretty big success, I think. I've heard that some stations wouldn't run it, because they believed it was too strong. Also, I understand that one tobacco company brought pressure that resulted in our parody of the Western shootout being taken off a West Coast station, and that was probably because the owners became persuaded that the line 'Cigarettes — they're killers' was too strong."

While the anti-cigarette forces were gradually mobilizing themselves, the tobacco industry was not idle. During the first quarter of 1969, the tobacco industry spent a good deal more money on television commercials than it had in the corresponding period of the previous year. On network television, the industry spent forty-five million three hundred thousand dollars for the quarter, as opposed to forty-three and a half million dollars for the first quarter of 1968, and its expenditures for spot announcements on individual stations rose by more than a million dollars, to a total of eleven million two hundred thousand dollars. Furthermore, most of this money was spent on advertising in prime time, in which the largest possible audiences could be reached.

With a very few exceptions — notably the Doyle Dane Bernbach and the Ogilvy & Mather agencies, which do not accept cigarette accounts — Madison Avenue appeared to remain pretty loyal to the tobacco industry. An article on the subject in February, 1969, in *Advertising Age* reported:

> A telephone check of 23 New York agencies [that do not have cigarette accounts], each large enough to absorb a sizable cigarette account without being absorbed by it, shows there are few that would decline one. Aside from long-time non-smokers like Doyle Dane Bernbach and Ogilvy & Mather, only four agencies in that [major-billing] category said that they would unequivocally be uninterested in a cigarette account — and two of those equivocated their unequivocal positions, suggesting that the offer, say, of $23,000,000 worth of Pall Mall business might bring about a quick change of policy. Top executives for each of the other 19 agencies replied, generally with no hesitation, that they would take on a cigarette account "gladly," "with pleasure," and "certainly."

The industry had also been doing its best — through the Tobacco Institute, which is its central trade organization and lobbying arm, in Washington — to persuade congressmen that there was nothing provably injurious about smoking cigarettes. With the help of the public-relations firm of Hill &

Knowlton, the Tobacco Institute also issued sheaves of press releases and background advisories, the gist of most of which was that the Surgeon General's report and the rest of the medical documents dealing with the relationship between smoking and lung cancer and other diseases were riddled with fallacies, and, in fact, were altogether unreliable. Then, in late 1967, the Tobacco Institute called up reinforcements, contracting for the services of the Tiderock Corporation, a sort of super-public-relations and management-consultant firm in New York.

The Tiderock Corporation was headed by Rosser Reeves, the ebullient former advertising man who for a number of years had been chairman of the board of the advertising agency Ted Bates & Co. and the undisputed prince of the hard sell in television advertising. At Ted Bates in the early fifties, Reeves had had a strong hand in promoting filter cigarettes, such as Viceroy and Kool, that were put out by Brown & Williamson. He had helped make the sales of these brands leap wildly with commercials containing such claims as "The nicotine and tars trapped by the exclusive Viceroy filter cannot reach your nose, throat, or lungs." (He later observed in connection with the medical studies on smoking and health that put the subject on the front pages in 1954, "We had already preempted the health kick.") Now Reeves, after having retired from the agency business and done some dealing in real estate down in Jamaica, had returned to Madison Avenue, set himself up in a suite of fifteen offices on the thirty-fifth floor of the Newsweek Building, and was consulting with half a dozen large corporate clients — "all big jungle cats, too," he said — on whatever public-relations or managerial problems afflicted them. I had an opportunity to interview Reeves on the subject of tobacco shortly after Tiderock took on the Tobacco Institute account, and although I gathered that the corporation was getting nearly half a million dollars for its services to tobacco, I never did get him to tell me exactly what it was doing for the Institute. However, I found him perfectly ready to say at some length that the tobacco industry had come in for much hard and unfair treatment at the hands of the federal government and of the medical people associated with the Surgeon General's report.

"After years of silence on the subject, the tobacco industry has decided that it is refreshing and necessary in any controversy to present both sides," Reeves told me. "I can say that I have been consulted on presenting the side of the controversy that has not been heard properly. The tobacco manufacturers do not claim that cigarettes do not cause cancer. They say very simply that it has not been proved that cigarettes *do* cause cancer. The question is still an open one. I *believe* that. You should see some of the crank letters I've got: I'm a merchant of death, I should be lashed to the stake. But I happen to be a very rich man — too rich to have to sell out for money."

Warming to the subject, Reeves continued, "I went to Washington. I looked into the propaganda machine of the federal bureaucracy and what it has been doing with the facts about smoking. For example, a study made for the Department of Health, Education, and Welfare, and published last May. Let me describe it. Volunteers are lined up. They call Mrs. A. They say, 'How old is your husband?' Or they get her daughter — the father isn't there, he's at work. 'How much does your father smoke?' 'Like a chimney.' 'How long has he

been smoking?' 'Forty years.' 'Does he cough?' 'All the time.'
'Worried about his heart?' 'Yes, as a matter of fact, his heart's
thumping.' 'Breathing?' 'He pants like an old locomotive.'
Wives and daughters turned into diagnosticians! And you just
try to get the raw data on that study, so that competent
statisticians can study it on computers. I'll bet you five
dollars to fifty thousand dollars you don't get it!"

Further: "The doctor is a layman in this matter. I gave a
cocktail party for fifteen top doctors. These are busy men.
We poured some gin into them. I told them, 'You know
about the smoking controversy.' 'Oh, yes, we've made a very
profound study.' And I found out that *not one* had read the
Surgeon General's report. They'd all got it from the *Times* or
the *News.*"

It was interesting to see a man who had made his fortune
out of commercials that habitually conjured up the authority
of medical science – doctors who were alleged to recommend
Anacin most when headaches strike; eminent skin specialists
who were supposed to attest to the glowing results for
women who carried out the Fourteen-Day Palmolive Beauty
Plan; eminent dental specialists whose studies were made to
demonstrate the clear superiority of Colgate Dental Cream –
suddenly fall upon the men in white and assail them as
deficient in scientific rigor. And it was interesting to see a
man who, in his advertising career, had shown such solicitude
for the public health that he mounted a vast campaign of
television commercials alerting the country to "doctors'
tests" proving that "Minute Maid Orange Juice is better for
your health than orange juice squeezed at home" now so
intent on playing down the dangers of smoking, and acting as
the chosen agent of the Tobacco Institute to attack the

Surgeon General of the United States for improper use of statistical method.

It was also interesting to see, some time after the Tobacco Institute obtained the services of Reeves' consulting organization, one result of this collaboration. In January, 1968, *True* carried an article entitled "To Smoke or Not to Smoke — That Is *Still* the Question," under the byline of Stanley Frank. The article took up the cause of the tobacco industry against the findings of the Surgeon General's report and other studies associating cigarette smoking with ill health, and it concluded, "At the moment, all we can say for sure is that the cause of cancer isn't known and that there is absolutely no proof that smoking causes human cancer."

Before its publication, the article was heavily promoted in advertisements appearing in the daily press, and a couple of months after publication it got even more publicity, slightly less favorable, when a story in the *Wall Street Journal* disclosed that Stanley Frank had become an employee of Hill & Knowlton, the public-relations people employed by the Tobacco Institute. It also disclosed that approximately six hundred and eight thousand reprints of the article had been sent out, most of them with a covering note signed "The Editors," to a list of "opinion-makers" throughout the country. But the reprints weren't sent out by the editors of *True*, even though they were printed on the presses of Fawcett Publications, which publishes *True*. They were sent out — and paid for — by none other than the Tiderock Corporation, which, it turned out, had also paid for the newspaper ads about the article. It was later disclosed that the "opinion-makers" who received the reprints included 184,647 doctors and other people in the field of medicine;

7,295 people in the communications field; 41,055 biological scientists; 18,819 educators; 10,142 government officials, including the 50 governors, 100 senators, and 432 representatives; 10,173 security analysts; and 123,779 other people, including lawyers, members of Junior Chambers of Commerce, and the like. In addition, three member companies of the Tobacco Institute — the American Tobacco Company, Philip Morris, and R.J. Reynolds — ordered directly from Fawcett two hundred thousand copies, sixty-five thousand one hundred copies and a hundred and thirty-five thousand copies, respectively, and, on top of this, Reynolds, Lorillard, Brown & Williamson, and Philip Morris obtained from the Tiderock Corporation a hundred thousand reprints of the article to send to their stockholders, company employees, and sales representatives. The Tobacco Institute and its members must have spent at least a hundred and seventy-five thousand dollars on the *True* project. Various complaints of unfair trade practices on the part of Tiderock, the Tobacco Institute, and the advertisements of the article were subsequently made to the Federal Trade Commission, and these resulted in an F.T.C. report to Congress. According to the report, which was submitted the following June, the *True* project had its genesis in discussions between Douglas Kennedy, then the editor of *True*, and a certain Joseph Field, whom the report identified as a public-relations man on retainer to Brown & Williamson. Field told the F.T.C. investigators that before and after the *True* article appeared he had sought to get national magazines to run articles presenting the tobacco industry's views on the subject of smoking and health, and he indicated that after his discussions with Douglas Kennedy, although he was given no commitment that such an article would be printed in *True*, he approached Stanley Frank, a free-lance writer for popular magazines who had done a number of articles for *True*, and paid him five hundred dollars to develop such an article. Approval of the idea, and reimbursement of the five hundred dollars, came from Brown & Williamson, Field said. Further inquiry revealed that Field then introduced Frank to an attorney for another tobacco company, and that this attorney supplied Frank with most of the material he used in writing the *True* article. The article was circulated among four *True* editors, two of whom thought it should be printed. A memorandum from a third editor responded less favorably: "Andy and Jack think this is great. I find it completely biassed and, if actually not hogwash, pretty damn misleading." A fourth editor found Frank's scientific critique of the Surgeon General's report and other medical documents somewhat surprising. He commented:

> If our old friend [name deleted in the F.T.C. report] had written this long, sob-sister plea for the tobacco industry I could at least understand his motives, but coming from Stanley Frank, a man who has spent many more years in baseball dugouts than in laboratories, I am at a loss . . . . Let's really face it: what's wrong here is that our writer didn't go out like a good reporter and do his legwork and his homework. The result is the purest trash — dated, biassed, and without present justification.

For the article, Frank was paid an author's fee of five hundred dollars and later additional payments totalling fifteen hundred dollars. (Frank went to work for Hill & Knowlton shortly before the appearance of the article in *True*, and he is still working there, but there is no evidence tying Hill & Knowlton to the *True* article. As a matter of fact, after the revelations about Tiderock's activities in publicizing the *True* article the Hill & Knowlton people were very unhappy.) Soon after the ramifications of the *True* article became public, Hill & Knowlton resigned the Tobacco Institute account. (Tiderock and the Tobacco Institute continued relations until the end of 1968.) Not unexpectedly, a number of liberal senators expressed shock at the tactics used by the Tiderock Corporation. However, Reeves' side of this little contretemps should be considered. He was doing his best to combat what he seemed to see as some vast new, Western-style doctors' plot against the tobacco manufacturers; the business of running an off-screen, print-oriented public-relations campaign was somewhat new to him, and probably, in his innocence, the former prince of the hard sell was merely trying to apply — as far as Tiderock's part in the *True* affair went — standards of addressing the public that are perfectly normal and acceptable in the world of television advertising.

Unfortunate as the revelations concerning the *True* article were for the tobacco industry, they were followed by even less welcome developments. In February, 1969, the Federal Communications Commission issued public notice that it intended to propose a ruling to ban cigarette advertising from all radio and television broadcasts. Because of "the hazard to public health" involved in cigarette smoking, it noted, the ruling was called for by the standard of public interest that broadcasters were legally obligated to adhere to. In taking this stand four months before the expiration date, on June 30, 1969, of those provisions in the Cigarette Labelling and

Advertising Act of 1965 which prohibited the F.C.C. and other regulatory agencies from taking action against tobacco advertising on the ground of health, the F.C.C. was plainly notifying Congress that it was prepared to move against cigarettes after June 30th if Congress didn't.

The tobacco-industry people were highly indignant at the F.C.C. statement of intention. The Tobacco Institute issued a statement declaring, "In the present state of scientific knowledge about smoking and health, the ruling contemplated by the F.C.C. would be arbitrary in the extreme." The broadcasters were indignant, too. Vincent T. Wasilewski, the president of the National Association of Broadcasters, issued a statement declaring, "The F.C.C. has arrogated to itself the formulation of a national policy . . . outside its field of expertise," and calling the policy one that should be left to Congress itself to determine. And Senator Sam J. Ervin, Jr., Democrat of North Carolina, the tobacco interests' senior defender in Congress, called the F.C.C. proposal "a supreme example of bureaucratic tyranny."

Thus, in the struggle over cigarette advertising the lines were drawn not only between the tobacco interests and the forces convinced of the dangers cigarette smoking presented to public health, and between the broadcasting interests and the F.C.C., but also between Congress and a regulatory agency.

Taking into account that, in addition to the F.C.C. proposal, the Federal Trade Commission had already made known, the previous year, not only its own opposition to the advertising of cigarettes on radio and television but also that it wished to require a stronger health warning on cigarette packs, the pro-tobacco forces realized that it was most important for them to concentrate on preventing the lapse of the preëmption clauses in the Cigarette Labelling and Advertising Act. Further, they knew that a number of bills proposing the restriction of tobacco sales and advertising were being processed in a number of states, and that if the preemption clauses of the Cigarette Labelling and Advertising Act did lapse, such bills might mushroom in every state and form a patchwork of regulations that would make nationally organized advertising and sales campaigns for cigarettes extremely difficult.

Consequently, great lobbying pressure was exerted by the pro-tobacco forces on members of the House Committee on Interstate and Foreign Commerce, which in April held hearings on various bills to amend the 1965 Cigarette Act, and on May 28th the committee, by a vote of twenty-two to five, reported out a bill, known as the Public Health Cigarette Smoking Bill, that would have extended the preëmption of any state- or federal-agency intervention against cigarette advertising for six years — a period longer by one-third than the moratorium built into the 1965 act. It looked like a clear victory for the tobacco forces, except for one tactical concession — a recommendation by the committee that a stronger health warning be required on cigarette packages. Instead of reading, "Caution: Cigarette Smoking May Be Hazardous to Your Health," the warning was now to read, "Warning: The Surgeon General Has Determined That Cigarette Smoking Is Dangerous to Your Health and May Cause Lung Cancer and Other Diseases." In arriving at this wording, the committee rejected a proposal from the Surgeon General himself that the last part of the warning read " . . . and May Cause Death from Cancer and Other Diseases." The word "death" made the tobacco people and their allies too unhappy. Even then, certain members of the committee felt that the modified warning was too much for them.

Since the label was not required to be placed on the front of the packages, this meant that it would continue to be put on one side, where it wouldn't be visible in cigarette commercials. And since the warning might conceivably help in some measure to relieve the tobacco companies of liability for damages arising out of lawsuits brought by the estates of deceased smokers who died of lung cancer, the tobacco men were unworried about this concession anyway.

The tobacco lobby was under the generalship of Earle C. Clements, a former Democratic senator from Kentucky, who was then president of the Tobacco Institute. His most active aides on Capitol Hill were Horace R. Kornegay, the Institute's current president and a former Democratic congressman from North Carolina, who until the previous year had had a seat on the House Interstate and Foreign Commerce Committee, and Jack Mills, former executive director of the Republican Congressional Campaign Committee. On Capitol Hill, Kornegay concentrated on the Democrats, Mills on the Republicans. The principal theme pursued by these lobbyists seemed to be that if the F.C.C. or the F.T.C. was allowed to ban or control the content of cigarette advertising, the agency would in effect be replacing congressional authority with administrative fiat, and would thereby be setting a dangerous precedent for restricting or banning all sorts of other legally sold products.

The tobacco lobbyists encouraged friends from other industries to see representatives and senators, too. "I've heard rumors that the tobacco people have been sending a member of the Liquor Institute around to see people on the Hill on their behalf," a lawyer close to the action told me not long before the House was preparing to vote on the cigarette bill. He added, "Madison Avenue is well represented here, too. The American Association of Advertising Agencies has a man sizing up the situation. He's getting something like a hundred grand a year. He has a broad mandate to find out what's going on, and he's around and about on the Hill. The individual tobacco companies have some high-priced legal talent watching the scene. The big Washington law firms are right in there – for example, Arnold & Porter, which is representing Philip Morris. These people know their way around Washington. The tobacco companies have other representatives here, too. One of the big tobacco companies has a fellow who, as I understand it, was once a private eye and was hired to catch up with Jimmy Hoffa's doings a few years ago. He's around, gathering intelligence. Then, there are all kinds of little fellows – free-lance lobbyists who sign on for a few bucks at one time or another. They'll drop in and make some inquiries for Earle Clements – that sort of thing. And then there are various people being hired whom we may not see directly – for example, fellows taken on to write position papers for the tobacco outfits. The tobacco people have been interested in recruiting some journalistic talent. A science reporter for one Washington paper told me a while ago of getting an offer of forty thousand dollars a year to go to work full time for the Tobacco Institute. The offer was turned down. Of course, Luke Quinn, who's the registered lobbyist for the American Cancer Society, is active on the Hill, too, and so is Banzhaf."

The broadcasting industry, with almost a quarter of a

billion dollars a year in cigarette-advertising accounts at
stake, was well represented in Washington during the legislative deliberations. "Vincent Wasilewski and other people
from the National Association of Broadcasters are very
active," I was told. "They're working closely with the
tobacco people. The broadcasters are able to bring a lot of
pressure to bear on the Hill. Congressmen don't like to
quarrel with broadcasters, and the broadcasters know that.
And on this issue the congressmen are hearing from their
local TV-station owners as well as from the N.A.B."

Apart from the argument that regulatory action on
cigarette advertising on the air would strengthen the agencies'
hand and thereby sap the power of Congress, the broadcasters maintained in their lobbying exercises that the
broadcasting industry itself was perfectly capable of regulating its advertising of legal products such as cigarettes, and in
fact, was *already* monitoring and regulating the cigarette
advertising that was offered it, through cigarette-advertising
guidelines devised by the Television Code Authority, the
administrative arm of the N.A.B.'s Television Code Review
Board. And it appeared that in deciding to stay the hand of
federal agencies bent on regulating cigarette advertising the
House committee had given considerable weight to the
testimony that Wasilewski offered concerning the self-
regulatory machinery established by the broadcasting industry. "The industry recognizes its obligation," Mr. Wasilewski
had assured the committee during its April hearings.
"Through [the Code Authority], it maintains a continuing
review of cigarette advertising on radio and television as it
relates to the public interest, and it has been responsive to
that interest. We believe that self-regulatory efforts have

played and are playing a significant role in dealing with the issue [of cigarette advertising], and that the furtherance of such efforts should be encouraged."

In mid-June, however, there was a development that showed these assurances in a different light, somewhat embarrassing to the broadcasting industry. Representative Brock Adams, of Washington, one of the five committee members who had voted against the tobacco interests, turned up evidence from Warren Braren, a former manager of the New York office of the Code Authority, on the extent of the N.A.B.'s self-regulation of cigarette advertising. On June 10th, Braren, who had become disillusioned by his working experience at the Code Authority, testified at a special committee hearing that whereas Congress had been informed that active and effective self-regulation existed in the N.A.B., the fact was that no such continuing review of cigarette commercials by the N.A.B. Code Authority people as Wasilewski had described currently existed, nor had existed since April, 1968, when a meeting between Wasilewski and other N.A.B. officials was held to discuss enforcement of the N.A.B. Code as it applied to cigarette advertising. As long ago as 1966, a confidential study made by the Code Authority staff had found that a good deal of cigarette advertising shown on the air could be construed as making smoking attractive and socially acceptable to young people, in violation of the Code Authority's publicly professed determination to see to it that in cigarette commercials "cigarette smoking not be depicted in a manner to impress the youth of our country as a desirable habit worthy of imitation." The study, he said, was in effect ignored by the N.A.B. Braren further testified that, subsequent to this study, resistance by television networks and tobacco companies to guidelines for the regulation of the content of tobacco advertising on the air — for example, a proposal to eliminate elements of cigarette commercials in which cigarette smoking was associated with virility and boy-girl romance or worldly success — had "disabled" the Code Authority, and it could no longer function effectively in policing cigarette advertising on the air. He said that when individual Code Authority members had suggested that the depiction of the act of smoking be abandoned in commercials, "President Wasilewski intervened with the argument that such a proscription was 'premature,' that it would drastically reduce the appeal of cigarette advertising, and consequently not be of benefit to broadcasters." The proposal for this restriction got nowhere. Braren said that in 1967 Code Authority members were cautioned by the Code Review Board not to be "too rigid" in interpreting the Code Authority's guidelines as they applied to specific commercials, and were advised by Clair McCollough, the board's chairman, that in arriving at a decision concerning the acceptability of cigarette commercials they should adhere to the standard of "When in doubt, O.K. it." Braren said that the coup de grâce was given the Code Authority's operations governing cigarette commercials when, at the April, 1968, meeting of N.A.B. officials, Stockton Helffrich, the Code Authority director, told staff members, "Network [affiliates] . . . see in the area of cigarette copy nothing to be achieved by Code Authority involvement and in fact [see] potential injury to cigarette-advertising revenue if the Code Authority pursues such a course."

To these charges both Wasilewski and Helffrich replied

before the House Interstate and Foreign Commerce Committee with general denials of negligence in formulating and enforcing workable guidelines to govern cigarette advertising on the air. And Braren's statements, though they might not have been much of a testimonial to the effectiveness of self-regulation by industry, had little effect on the pro-tobacco momentum that had been built up in the House of Representatives through vigorous lobbying. On June 18th, the cigarette bill came to a vote on the floor of the House. "Tobacco interests were in firm control throughout the House voting as anti-smoking forces were beaten in every attempt to reshape the measure," the *Times* reported the following day. The House passed the bill by a voice vote.

The bill was now sent to the Senate, but its reception in the appropriate committee there was far less friendly than it had been in the House Interstate and Foreign Commerce Committee. Senator Warren G. Magnuson, Democrat of Washington, the politically powerful chairman of the full Senate Committee on Commerce, was on record as being in favor of restrictions on cigarette advertising. Two years previously, he and Senator Robert F. Kennedy had jointly proposed to the major tobacco companies that they allow their cigarette commercials to be broadcast only after ten o'clock at night. Furthermore, the chairman of the Commerce Committee's Consumer Subcommittee, which would be holding hearings on the cigarette bill, was Frank E. Moss, Democrat of Utah, who represented a large number of Mormons, who are non-smokers. For his own part, Senator Moss was so firmly opposed to cigarette advertising on radio and television that he had already promised to filibuster, if necessary, against any Senate bill that would prohibit federal agencies from regulating or banning it. On top of all this, the annual report to Congress of the Federal Trade Commission was due. In 1968, the F.T.C.'s annual report had recommended that a strong warning to the effect that cigarette smoking may "cause death" be placed on all cigarette packages and included in all cigarette advertising and that cigarette advertising be banned from radio and television entirely. And this year the F.T.C. was expected to press these recommendations very hard. In fact, when the report was sent to Congress, early in July, it not only repeated these recommendations but also recommended that broadcasters be required, as part of their public-service responsibilities, to devote a significant amount of broadcasting time to programs and announcements on the health hazards of cigarette smoking. Once again, too, there was the threat that the F.C.C. would intervene directly — unless the Senate as well as the House acted to prevent it — to ban cigarette advertising from the air.

Having taken all these circumstances into account, the broadcasters came up with a plan that they thought might forestall the threat from the federal regulators. Around the time of the F.T.C. report, a deputation of broadcasters made a visit to Senator Magnuson's office and advanced a proposal that had been conceived by network policy-makers, at N.B.C.'s Washington office. Under the N.B.C. scheme, the networks would gradually phase out advertising for the cigarette brands that had the highest tar and nicotine content,thus eventually limiting the cigarette advertising they carried to the low-tar-and-nicotine brands. They proposed this on the theory that the promotion of low-tar-and-nicotine cigarettes was less objectionable to opponents of cigarette advertising than the promotion of the high-tar-and-nicotine variety. The plan was also in accord with a suggestion that Magnuson himself had once made in regard to limiting cigarette advertising. It was also in accord with the economic interests of the network people, who were calculating that whatever changes might take place in the budgets assigned by the tobacco companies to high- and low-tar-and-nicotine brands, the total revenues from cigarette advertising had a chance of remaining more or less intact.

This plan was a tempting one to Senator Magnuson, not only because it was in line with his own prior proposal but also because, if he were to accept it, a great deal of wrangling between the Senate and the House on the subject of tobacco advertising could be prevented. For help in evaluating the plan, Magnuson sent the chief counsel of the Senate Commerce Committee, Michael Pertschuk, a lawyer in his mid-thirties, who has a reputation on Capitol Hill of being an extremely knowledgeable man on consumer-affairs legislation, to Dr. Daniel Horn, coauthor with Dr. E. Cuyler Hammond of the widely publicized report in 1954 that associated cigarette smoking with the incidence of lung cancer and other diseases. Dr. Horn had been appointed director of the National Clearinghouse on Smoking and Health, an organ of the United States Public Health Service, when it was set up in 1965. Throughout the battle over smoking and health, Magnuson had admired Dr. Horn's ability to assess not only the scientific but also the social problems involved in the continuation of this mass habit. Dr. Horn himself believed that if an outright ban on cigarette advertising could not be achieved, confining the advertising that *was* done to low-tar-and-nicotine brands had some value, since his own research on smoking habits had shown that for some habitual smokers a switch from high- to low-tar-and-nicotine cigarettes was a way station toward ridding themselves of the habit altogether. Nevertheless, Dr. Horn told Pertschuk, whatever value the N.B.C. plan might have in keeping high-tar cigarettes from being advertised on the air, it would in his opinion be entirely offset by the depiction of the act of smoking in those commercials that *were* put on the air. Horn's studies showed that viewing this act had an unhinging effect on the resolution of people who were trying to cut out smoking. Next, Horn reviewed the supposed advantages of the low-tar scheme against the background of what he said was a growing public conviction that cigarette smoking really was harmful to health, and pointed out that many smokers were adjusting their smoking habits accordingly. He said that while he thought confining cigarette advertising to the promotion of low-tar-and-nicotine brands might seem a reasonable interim solution to the regulatory problem, the problem was really not a regulatory or scientific one but one of morality: Should the United States government accept the promotion of a habit that had been proved so devastating to the nation's health? After thinking things over, Magnuson decided that the low-tar-and-nicotine advertising scheme wasn't an adequate way of coping with the problem.

At that point, both Senator Magnuson and Senator Moss exerted strong pressure on the broadcasters to come up with more far-reaching concessions on cigarette advertising. They seem to have also taken deft advantage of cracks that were beginning to appear in the lobbying alliance between the broadcasters and the tobacco manufacturers. The tobacco people were taken aback by the behavior of the broadcasters in proposing a phaseout of high-tar-and-nicotine advertising. "The conversations of the broadcasters on this matter were in secret. I can't understand their not explaining their intentions to the cigarette industry," a staff member of the Tobacco Institute told me in discussing this development. The tobacco men had another complaint, too. In spite of all the advertising talk about "mildness," many tobacco merchandisers considered the most successful brands of cigarettes on the market to be those with higher, rather than lower, tar and nicotine content. And since the most successful brands were those into which the most promotional and marketing money had already been poured, brand managers in the cigarette business now predicted unhappily that scores of millions of promotional dollars that had been spent on television campaigns for particular high-tar brands would be spent in vain if the broadcasters' plan went through.

The broadcasters denied that they had been negotiating in secret to the detriment of their friends in the tobacco business. "The tobacco people knew all along what we were doing, but *we've* never known what *they* were doing," a man who was involved in the negotiations for the broadcasters told me. In spite of the broadcasters' protestations that they were keeping the tobacco manufacturers informed of their political negotiations, the tobacco manufacturers were in for a further shock. Under pressure from the Senate, and out of fear that if federal regulatory agencies stepped in to do something about cigarette advertising on the air a great deal of advertising for other products might suffer the same fate, the broadcasters gave in. On July 8th, the National Association of Broadcasters, through its Television Code Review Board, announced a plan to phase out not only high-tar-and-nicotine cigarette advertising but all kinds of cigarette advertising from the air over a three-and-a-half-year period beginning January 1, 1970. It was a very heavy blow to the tobacco men, who now saw that their cause, as far as radio and television were concerned, was lost. Even the three and a half years over which the phaseout was to be extended gave them no satisfaction; as far as the respective competitive positions of individual tobacco companies were concerned, it was clear that over this phaseout period the plan would favor the sales of those brands that were then in a dominant position in the market and place at a disadvantage the less powerful companies that were trying to dislodge them by putting large advertising sums into their own brands. The tobacco companies thus fell to quarrelling among themselves. They now seemed united only in their resentment of what they viewed as a sellout by their old friends the broadcasters, to whom they had given such vast sums over the years for cigarette advertising.

Already, the tobacco men had been discussing among themselves what contingency measures they might have to adopt to head off a situation in which they might be forced by federal regulators to put a health warning on every kind of cigarette advertising, including print ads. The disarray of the tobacco people was compounded as a result of a declaration made by their own representative at a hearing of the Federal Trade Commission on July 2nd concerning the propriety of requiring a health warning to be included in all cigarette advertising. At the hearing, Thomas Austern, of the powerful Washington law firm of Covington & Burling, who was representing the Tobacco Institute, advanced the argument that any such warning in cigarette advertising was unnecessary, because all the publicity given in the mass media — including the anti-smoking commercials — to the issue of smoking and health "demonstrates that the current public awareness of the hazard in cigarette smoking is now patent." "You say everybody knows that cigarette smoking is dangerous to health?" Commissioner Philip Elman asked the Tobacco Institute counsel.

"Yes. I will take it on that issue, sir," Austern replied, indicating that he intended to use this premise in his argument, and he did.

After all the years and all the millions of dollars that the industry had devoted to denying the validity of the individual reports of these hazards, this was a horrifying argument for the tobacco men to see reported in the news. It was so horrifying, in fact, that one official of the Tobacco Institute with whom I hoped to discuss the subject a month later reacted to my mention of it as though the Institute's counsel had never advanced such an argument at all. He was the Institute's public-relations director, and he may have just blocked it out of his mind.

Whatever the tobacco people felt about Mr. Austern's characterization of the effects of cigarettes on smokers, there was no doubt that they were increasingly worried about the effects of anti-smoking commercials on smokers and on potential smokers. "The anti-smoking spots are dreadfully effective," a staff member of the Tobacco Institute remarked to me one day that summer, and a few days later a former executive of a major tobacco company who had just been removed from his organization as a result of a corporate merger, and was consequently feeling a bit disillusioned about the tobacco business, told me, "The industry considers that the anti-smoking commercials, on top of the tremendous anti-smoking campaigns that have been mounted in the public schools by the Public Health Service and the various health organizations, and this on top of all the other unfavorable publicity about smoking, are really hurting. In fact, the opinion of many top-level tobacco people is that as things stand they'd just as soon have cigarette commercials banned altogether if by that they could in effect get the anti-smoking commercials banned, too." Whatever their considerations were, the tobacco forces rallied themselves for a heavy counterstroke against the broadcasters. On July 22nd, at a hearing of the Senate Commerce Committee's Consumer Subcommittee, Joseph F. Cullman III, head of Philip Morris, promised, on behalf of the nine leading cigarette manufacturers in the country, to end all cigarette advertising on radio and television not by the 1973 deadline proposed by the broadcasters but by September, 1970. He attached only one condition to this pledge — that Congress grant the tobacco manufacturers immunity in this case from the anti-trust laws, under which they might be charged with restraining trade by thus acting in concert.

Cullman went even further. He informed the subcommittee that if the broadcasters would release the tobacco manufacturers from their existing advertising contracts, the tobacco manufacturers would be prepared to withdraw their cigarette commercials from the air by January 1, 1970. "This was a very smart move on the part of the tobacco forces," a man on the subcommittee told me. "Suddenly the tobacco companies were putting themselves in a heroic role. According to them, it was now only the greed of the networks that was keeping cigarette commercials on TV. Actually, the companies were angling for a lot more than a P.R. gesture. What they were really after now was legislation that would ostensibly be aimed at getting cigarette commercials off the air but would actually protect the tobacco industry by forbidding the F.T.C. to require it to put a health warning in all tobacco ads. And, in fact, the tobacco people's chances of forestalling that mandatory health warning did begin to look better."

The broadcasters were aggrieved. They had not expected this drastic move by the tobacco people, and they were particularly put out by the manner in which the tobacco men had somehow managed to throw a mantle of statesmanship over themselves. Worse still, an advance of the deadline from September of 1973 to September of 1970 for removing cigarette commercials from the air was going to cost the broadcasters perhaps a third of a billion dollars in advertising revenue, the amount depending on the terms of a proposed phaseout. "We helped the tobacco people throughout this fight, and they pulled the rug out from under us," a man who had taken a leading part in formulating the broadcasting industry's strategy in Washington told me. "The thing that irks us is that the tobacco people couldn't have got the bill through the House without our help. We really lobbied for that. It would *never* have passed the House without us, because we have more muscle than the tobacco people have. There are a hell of a lot more broadcasters than cigarette manufacturers in this country. In every congressman's district, there is at least one broadcaster. These congressmen all get exposure on the local TV and radio stations, by making periodic reports to their constituents over the stations on all sorts of matters — what they've been doing about farm legislation, pollution, taxes, and so on. I know how hard we worked through our local broadcasters on this bill, pointing out to congressmen how unfair it was to ban advertising for a product sold legally, how unfair it was to discriminate against one medium of advertising in favor of another, and so on. We put in a *lot* of work. And the tobacco people left us in the lurch."

What the broadcasters found particularly galling was the notion that the quarter of a billion dollars a year they had been getting for cigarette advertising was going to wind up in someone else's hands, and that at least some of it might wind up in the hands of their competitors in the newspapers and magazines, from whom the broadcasters had wrested the greater part of cigarette-advértising revenue years ago. The idea that the tobacco people would abandon them so abruptly in exchange for a chance at arranging a *modus vivendi* with these competing media was too much. "If the tobacco people think they're going to use the broadcasting industry as a pawn to get protection in other media from labelling legislation, that's something we won't sit still for," an official of the National Association of Broadcasters told me shortly after the tobacco interests had delivered their counterblow.

Moving into the breach between the former allies, Senator Moss sent off letters to the heads of the three television networks suggesting that they voluntarily release the tobacco companies from their existing advertising contracts, so that, in the public interest, all cigarette commercials could be withdrawn from the air by January 1, 1970. This suggestion was not received with enthusiasm at the networks. Dr. Frank Stanton, the president of C.B.S., replied to Senator Moss, "If Congress determines that the permissive legislation sought by the Tobacco Institute is in the public interst, C.B.S. will release the cigarette advertisers from their commitments" – which was perhaps a public-spirited way of saying that any advertiser who wanted to withdraw his cigarette commercials from C.B.S. by January 1, 1970, would have to do it by act of Congress, because C.B.S. wasn't volunteering to do the job on its own. Dr. Stanton went on to ask, most unkindly as far as the tobacco advertisers were concerned:

> If the public interest should require legislation in this area, should not the legislation deal with the problem as a whole and not direct its restraints only against the television and radio media? To put it another way, if the product is considered sufficiently dangerous to ban from one form of advertising, should it not be outlawed entirely?

As for N.B.C., its president, Julian Goodman, expressed himself as being sincerely sorry that he could not comply with Senator Moss's suggestion. He wrote that if broadcasters dropped cigarette commercials by the following January 1st, "a severe drop in revenue" and consequent "changes in the program service available to the public" would result. "Therefore, we do not intend to release cigarette advertisers from their existing commitments," he wrote. He added that N.B.C. would, however, be "glad to cooperate" with the tobacco companies by accepting, after January, 1970, in lieu of cigarette commercials, commercials for any goods besides cigarettes that the tobacco companies might be producing.

The president of A.B.C., Leonard H. Goldenson, said no,

too. He wrote that taking cigarette commercials off the air by January 1st in the manner suggested would be unfair and expensive, explaining:

> If we did take such action as of January, 1970, it could well mean a substantial cutback in our news and public-affairs operations almost immediately and would also call for a complete reexamination of all other program commitments to see whether or not a full schedule of the present magnitude could be maintained. We do not believe that the Congress would look with favor on any such forced curtailment of network service to the American public.

In short, A.B.C. owed it to the public to keep the cigarette commercials on the tube. As things were, A.B.C.'s going rate for cigarette commercials run in prime time was forty thousand dollars a minute, and, looking ahead to the prospect of tobacco-company sponsorship for the 1970 professional-football season, the network was setting an asking price of sixty-five thousand dollars a minute for cigarette commercials run during the games.

If the broadcasters were displaying withdrawal symptoms in the matter of phaseout, many of their colleagues in the newspaper and magazine business were apparently feeling no pain. According to an article in *Advertising Age* on July 28th, Stephen Kelly, the president of the Magazine Publishers Association, said in an interview that while he couldn't speak for all magazines, there was "some substance" to the suggestion that there would be a rush among magazine advertising departments to pick up at least some of the cigarette-advertising revenue that the broadcasters were going to lose. The article in *Advertising Age* also described Jack Kauffman, the president of the Bureau of Advertising of the

American Newspaper Publishers Association, as "openly optimistic" about the cigarette-ad prospects of newspaper publishers. It quoted Kauffman as saying enthusiastically that "newspapers will be the chief beneficiary" of a pullout of cigarette advertising from radio and television, and that there had "definitely been movement" in this respect.

In the magazine business, certainly, there was no discernible movement away from cigarette advertising. A spokesman for *Newsweek* who was asked by a reporter for the *Wall Street Journal* whether his publication had any plans for changing its cigarette-advertising policies said, "We feel that we've covered fully the story of the alleged hazards of cigarette smoking, and we assume people have heard and read all they possibly could on the subject and have made up their own minds. We've always taken cigarette ads and will continue to do so." Some time after this statement was issued, John T. Landry, a Philip Morris man whose title is Group Vice-President and Director of Marketing for Tobacco Products, was quoted as having told a group of ad men that representatives from the advertising departments of various publications were showing up at the headquarters of tobacco companies as if it were a scene "like the reading of the will."

In an effort to determine the attitude of magazine publishers toward accepting an increased volume of cigarette advertising — or accepting any cigarette advertising at all — Senator Moss wrote letters to a number of them asking for their views. The publishers' replies were not much more encouraging than the broadcasters' had been. A letter from Andrew Heiskell, the chairman of Time Inc., set the general tone. "It would not be in the public interest or our own for us arbitrarily to refuse to carry the responsible advertising of a lawful product," Mr. Heiskell informed Senator Moss. He added, however, that his company did not intend to surfeit its readers with an "overwhelming" amount of cigarette advertising. In the magazine business generally, the publications that already had a policy of not accepting cigarette advertising were few in number. They included the *Reader's Digest* (which had an exemplary record of printing articles having to do with the dangers of smoking), the *Saturday Review*, and *The New Yorker*.

As for the newspaper publishers, no matter what their editorials might have been saying about smoking and health, or how dispassionately they had viewed the plight of the broadcasters faced with the issue of smoking and health, they showed, on the whole, that they had no intention of eliminating cigarette advertising, or even of turning away further revenues that might follow the proposed cutoff of cigarette commercials from the airwaves. There were very few exceptions. They included the *Christian Science Monitor*, which had never carried cigarette advertising and had no intention of carrying it, and the Boston *Globe*, whose management announced in May, 1969, that it would no longer accept such advertising, "because accumulated medical evidence has indicated that cigarette smoking is hazardous to health." In the months after the tobacco people caved in on cigarette commercials, the most important newspaper to alter its policy on cigarette ads was the *New York Times*. On August 29th, the *Times* ran an editorial saying, "In advance of the steps we hope Congress will take to establish tighter health safeguards by law, the *Times* is taking voluntary action to insure that a health warning accompanies any cigarette advertisements it carries." As of January 1, 1970, it explained, the paper would accept cigarette ads only if they contained, "in plainly legible form," a warning concerning the health hazards of smoking.

The tobacco industry's reaction to this move was made clear by a full-page ad that the American Tobacco Company took in the *Times*, on September 4th. The headline on the ad read, in huge letters, "**WHY WE'RE DROPPING THE NEW YORK TIMES**." The text of the ad declared that the American Tobacco Company had "offered" to take its commercials off television and radio because of "the claim that those media unavoidably reach large numbers of children," and "not because we agree with anti-cigarette crusaders (including the *New York Times*) who would like to blame cigarettes for the thousand and one ills that flesh is heir to." Hard on this belligerent declaration, spokesmen for Liggett & Myers, R.J. Reynolds, the Lorillard Corporation, Philip Morris, and Brown & Williamson made it known that they did not intend to advertise their cigarettes in the *Times*, either, under the conditions prescribed.

The broadcasters, for their part, kept hammering away at the tobacco industry and the press alike, going so far as to make common cause with the federal regulators who had been partly responsible for depriving them of huge potential cigarette-commercial revenues. In October, Wasilewski complained in a letter to Senator Moss in connection with the "discriminatory legislation" proposed by the tobacco industry that "there are indications that large sums of money would be diverted by the cigarette companies from broadcast advertising to promote their products by other means," and that it appeared that "vast expenditures could be made for promotional programs employing such devices as coupons, premiums, contests, point-of-sale promotion, and samples" as well as advertising in print. Helpfully, Wasilewski enclosed a news clipping from the Washington *Sunday Star* that, he wrote, "states that no change is contemplated in the current level of tobacco subsidies of fifty million dollars per year and that $230,000 will be spent annually [on subsidies] for *advertising* of tobacco products in friendly foreign countries." And he concluded that, rather than see Congress act on the tobacco companies' proposal, the broadcasters would prefer to have the regulation of cigarette advertising handled by the regulatory agencies.

Amid all this dissension between the formerly inseparable partners in the mass merchandising of cigarettes, the full Commerce Committee, headed by Senator Magnuson, met in October to consider amendments to the House bill governing cigarette advertising on the air. The committee voted an amendment to make mandatory the withdrawal of cigarette commercials from television and radio. Senator Philip A. Hart, Democrat of Michigan, a member of the committee and a strong supporter of anti-trust legislation, had persuaded the committee that it would be unwise to accept the terms of the tobacco industry's offer to withdraw its advertising from the air by September, 1970 — unwise because the exemption from the anti-trust laws which the industry asked as a condition might prove to be a legal booby trap that could damage future enforcement of the anti-trust laws. The best the broadcasters could get from the committee on this point, though, was a concession in the form of an amendment that would make the ban on cigarette commercials effective not by September of 1970, as the tobacco people had proposed, but by January 1, 1971 — the idea being to let the broadcasters have the benefit of a final shower of cash from the cigarette revenues generated by the fall football season.

The lobbyists for the tobacco industry had a little better luck with members of the committee than the broadcasters had. "The tobacco people were very busy," a committee staff member told me. "They moved in on the committee and managed to carry two amendments that favored them. First, they won a statutory provision that would prohibit the Federal Trade Commission from acting on the health warning in cigarette ads for eighteen months after the termination of cigarette advertising on the air — which meant that they forced an extension by a whole year of a deadline that the F.T.C. had in the meantime set for requiring a health warning in all cigarette ads. Then the tobacco lobby swung enough votes in the committee to bring about a change in the text of the existing warning label required on cigarette packages. At first, the committee (bypassing the text required in the House bill) decided to alter the text of the existing warning on cigarette packages from "Caution: Cigarette Smoking May be Hazardous to Your Health" to "Warning: Cigarette Smoking Is Dangerous to Your Health." When the tobacco lobbyists learned about that, they put enough pressure on so that the committee changed its mind and, by a narrow vote, further amended the notice to read, "Warning: Excessive Cigarette Smoking is Dangerous to Your Health." That was a considerable gain for the tobacco lobby, because the use of the word "excessive" made the warning imply that *normal* smoking *wasn't* dangerous to health — which was not what the Surgeon General's report had said. What the Surgeon General's report had said was that cigarette smoking in normal amounts was indeed dangerous to health.

The amended bill came to a vote in the Senate on December 12th. Before it did, Senators Magnuson and Moss had launched a battle against the denatured health warning on the cigarette packages, and won. Through further amendments, they obtained the elimination of the word "excessive," and they also managed to have reduced by one year the period during which the F.T.C. was forbidden to require a health warning in all cigarette advertising. The F.T.C. could require this warning, after giving Congress six months' notice of its intention to do so, after July 1, 1971. In addition, the Commission would be permitted to impose certain other requirements on cigarette advertising, such as that the tar and nicotine content of the brands concerned be included. The bill was passed by a vote of seventy to seven. It was then sent to House and Senate conferees for a resolution of differences between the two versions. The broadcasters went to work on the conferees in a final attempt to delay the cutoff date for cigarette commercials to September, 1971. What they finally got was a delay of one day — from midnight of December 31, 1970 to midnight of January 1, 1971 — which enabled them to cash in on cigarette commercials during the football bowl games on New Year's Day. The victory was a far cry from the millions of dollars that a nine-month extension would have given the broadcasters, but it was something.

And the broadcasters had not yet finished with the tobacco people. Now that there wasn't going to be so much money to be made out of cigarette commercials, the broadcasters began to think that there might, after all, be an ethical issue involved in promoting cigarettes. After Braren's revelations, the N.A.B. Code Authority people hastily went through the motions of tightening up their cigarette-advertising guidelines, and in December the American Tobacco Company tried to get a court injunction to prevent the N.A.B. from adopting certain of these guidelines, whereupon an N.A.B. lawyer collecting depositions from witnesses at a pre-trial hearing put a long series of questions concerning the morality of advertising cigarettes to Philip Cohen, director of advertising for American Tobacco. Attorneys for American Tobacco would allow Cohen to answer only one of them, which was put to him by a lawyer representing C.B.S. and ran as follows: "In preparing advertising, do you assume that there is a relationship between smoking and health, or do you assume there is no relationship?" Cohen replied, "We don't make any assumptions. We prepare advertising that is calculated to sell the market."

On April 1, 1970, the Public Health Cigarette Smoking Act was at last signed into law by President Nixon. In form, it had been changed very little in the House-Senate conference, but the wording of the cautionary label on cigarette packages had again been altered. It now read, "Warning: The Surgeon General Has Determined that Cigarette Smoking is Dangerous to Your Health."

Twenty years ago, when television was just getting under way in this country and the tobacco companies were beginning to pour big money into commercials, advertising men in the Madison Avenue agencies that had cigarette accounts were working full tilt to convert themselves from the static visual forms of printed advertising to the visual and aural mobility of the new medium. Young copywriters who had been yanked away from the preparation of cigarette ads for the magazines rushed around talking about "iris wipes," "barn-door wipes," and other techniques for "videoizing" the usual advertising forms. But since the passage of the Public Health Cigarette Smoking Act, things have been swinging the other way in the agencies with cigarette accounts. Ad men on cigarette accounts who have been almost entirely television-oriented throughout their professional careers are beginning to be heard discussing "bleed pages" and "double trucks." They are beginning to be aware of color shots that don't show motion but only still slices of motion, of copy that isn't audible, of printed words that aren't meant to zoom in at viewers but are designed merely to sit still on a page. An increase in the number of cigarette ads in certain mass magazines is already apparent. For example, the October 16, 1970, issue of *Life* contained five full-page cigarette ads, four of them (including the back cover) in color, in contrast to the October 17, 1969, issue, which contained only three full-page cigarette ads.

However eager some publishers appear to be to solicit cigarette advertising from the tobacco companies, it is not likely that they will have reason to exult for long at having taken away advertising from the television people. The television networks, which stand to lose approximately eight percent of their total annual advertising revenue through the Public Health Cigarette Smoking Act, are now attempting to avenge the loss of their tobacco advertising by unleashing their time salesmen upon ad agencies to grab all manner of other consumer-product advertising revenue from the print media, whose own resulting losses may turn out to be greater than whatever gain they may enjoy from cigarette advertising. How much more advertising money than formerly the tobacco companies are putting into the print media as a whole is as yet unclear. But there are practical considerations that make it unlikely that this increase will be a startling one. The tobacco people have to be aware of the fact that escalation of print advertising is a very dangerous game for them, since a marked rise in cigarette ads in publications would almost certainly provoke action by the Federal Trade Commission to require the inclusion of a health warning in those ads published after the new deadline, and such a requirement is what the tobacco industry dreads most. Rather than risk putting too much cigarette-advertising money into publications, the industry will probably spread its ad money around in other areas. For example, it will probably increase the amount of money it spends on point-of-purchase advertising and promotion — more elaborate displays in supermarkets, and so forth. In less visible moves, the tobacco people can spend more money on their sales forces that deal with cigarette retailers, and offer bigger sales incentives to both wholesalers and retailers. They can go in for special cigarette-brand promotions, in areas like sports. Thus, Philip Morris is underwriting a series of tournaments for women tennis players, to be known as the Virginia Slims Invitational Tournament Series. (Presumably, the progress of the tournaments will be reported on television, and viewers will thus continue to hear the words "Virginia Slims" over the tube.) Outside the magazines and newspapers, the most visible use of the television-commercial money will be on outdoor billboards. It has been estimated in the trade that in 1971 the tobacco companies will spend as much as forty million dollars on billboard advertising — an increase of a thousand percent over the amount they spent on billboard advertising in 1970.

Whatever the tobacco companies spend on printed advertising and on other forms of promotion, it will not come to anything like the quarter of a billion dollars a year that they have been spending on radio and television. It appears that the elimination of cigarette advertising from broadcast media represents, among other things, an enforced levelling of the costs of competing companies, and an opportunity for the industry to forgo the huge and unrelenting escalation of expenses that occurred during the tobacco-merchandising wars on network television. Without broadcast advertising, the introduction of new brands into the market — a process that is already extremely expensive for individual cigarette manufacturers (it may take as much as twelve million dollars to launch a new brand of cigarettes nationally) — is likely to be even more difficult, and is therefore likely to slow up. An end to the wild proliferation of new brands will certainly cut the expenses of competing companies. Also, the tobacco companies may be spared some of the dagger blows now being dealt them by the anti-smoking commercials. When cigarette commercials go off the air, the broadcasters, no matter how strongly they feel about their former friends in the cigarette industry, will no longer consider themselves bound under the F.C.C. fairness doctrine to grant the anti-smoking forces, free of charge, that seventy-five million dollars' worth of air time a year, and it is certain that there will be a considerable falling off in the amount of time given over to the anti-smoking messages. With such developments, the elimination of cigarette commercials from radio and television may before long result in an increase rather than a decrease in the profits of the cigarette industry on each of the billions of cartons being sold per year.

But if the tobacco companies may collect bonuses of this sort from the elimination of broadcast cigarette advertising, the gains will not necessarily prove lasting. It seems to me that the long-term prospects for the cigarette industry are not favorable. One can begin with what has been happening to cigarette sales. Since 1963, the year before the Surgeon General's report, the total number of cigarettes sold in this country has increased from seventy-one million eight hundred thousand packs a day in that calendar year (in 1963, cigarette sales had been higher than at any previous point in smoking history) to seventy-two million six hundred thousand packs a day in the year ending July 1, 1970. This rise in total sales is, relatively speaking, a small one, because in those six and a half years the adult population of the United States has increased by thirteen million people. Thus, while the number of adults in the country has gone up by about ten percent, cigarette sales have gone up by only about one percent. This means that the per-capita consumption of cigarettes in the adult population has actually gone down by nearly nine percent. But even this per-capita drop does not tell the whole story, because in this same six-and-a-half-year period the total production of tobacco itself, as distinct from the total number of cigarettes sold, has dropped from two billion three hundred and forty-four million pounds to one billion eight hundred million pounds — a decrease of about twenty percent. Some, but not very much, of this decrease may be accounted for by new processing methods, such as the "homogenizing" of formerly discarded tobacco-leaf stems and their incorporation into the finished cigarette. Essentially, the decrease appears to result from the fact that the tobacco companies have been packing considerably less tobacco into their cigarettes than they formerly did, even though their cigarettes have tended to get longer. What seems to have filled up most of this cigarette gap is more filter material, which, as it happens, is considerably cheaper per centimeter of cigarette than tobacco is, and which, given the right advertising agency, can be merchandised — in hundred-millimeter cigarettes, for example — at higher prices. In summary, then, what has happened since 1963 is that the total amount of cigarette tobacco per capita consumed by the adult population has fallen off by close to twenty percent, and that in return for this the tobacco companies have been selling slightly more cigarettes, containing considerably less tobacco, more filter, and more air, at higher prices than ever.

But the less actual tobacco people smoke, the less stubborn their habituation to cigarettes tends to be. It seems inescapable that in spite of the huge momentum that the tobacco industry has achieved in promoting cigarettes over the past half century, using every medium of mass persuasion, including television (into which it has poured a total of perhaps three billion dollars of advertising money in twenty years), the whole pattern of cigarette smoking within the adult population is now changing significantly. Dr. Horn has calculated that between 1966 and 1970 the total number of smokers in the adult population has dropped from forty-nine million to forty-four and a half million. At the same time, his calculations indicate, the number of former smokers in the adult population has risen from nineteen million to twenty-nine million. Dr. Horn estimates that since 1966 one smoker in five has quit the habit. And although at an earlier period — for example, in the period immediately after the Surgeon

General's 1964 report on smoking and health – most people who cut out the habit tended to be above average in education and earning power, Dr. Horn believes that giving up the cigarette habit is now occurring at increasing rates in the adult population generally, and that it is occurring at significant levels among women as well as among men (although women smokers appear to have a harder time quitting than men), and also among younger adults, although there seems to have been a slight increase in the smoking rate among teenagers during the last two years.

When one takes into account all the commercial force that the tobacco companies have brought to bear in our society over the years to promote brands of cigarettes, and all the lobbying they have done, and all the influence they have exerted on one Administration and one Congress after another, and when one reflects that although the total excess deaths among regular smokers since the time of the Surgeon General's report in 1964 must be numbered in the hundreds of thousands, the tobacco and broadcasting people were nonetheless able for so long to persuade the House of Representatives to vote a ban on effective regulation of cigarette advertising on the air, this change is a remarkable one. The tobacco manufacturers cannot but be aware of it. However obdurate their leaders have been in public in denying the harmfulness of cigarette smoking, and however determined they are to continue promoting cigarettes by every means at their disposal, the tobacco companies have been steadily diversifying their activities over the past two or three years. The American Tobacco Company has become a subsidiary of American Brands, Inc., and besides manufacturing Pall Mall, Tareyton, Lucky Strike, and Silva Thins cigarettes it manufactures a number of food products, including Sunshine Crackers and Cookies, Mott's Fruits and Fruit Juices, and Sunsweet Fruits and Fruit Juices, and has announced its intention of taking over the Jergens Company, which puts out Jergens Lotion and Woodbury Soap. Two of the largest tobacco companies have dropped the word "tobacco" from their corporate names. Thus, the Liggett & Myers Tobacco Co. has become just Liggett & Myers, Inc., and in addition to making L & M, Lark, and Chesterfield cigarettes it now puts out Alpo Dog Foods and Cream of Oats. And the R.J. Reynolds Tobacco Company recently changed its name to R.J. Reynolds Industries, Inc. The renamed company, as it continues to proclaim that Winston tastes good like a cigarette should, is also pushing the taste of such products as Chun King Oriental foods, Hawaiian Punch, Brer Rabbit Molasses, and My-T-Fine desserts, which it now also manufactures. The Brown & Williamson Tobacco Corporation retains its name, but it is now in the pickled-fish business as well as in the tobacco business.

On the whole, the manufacture and promotion of cigarettes are likely to be highly profitable for some time. But tobacco companies that will have diversified to the point where their tobacco products are no longer their major source of income will not be likely, if they are faced with financial problems, to make many sacrifices for the sake of a product whose sales aren't expanding, particularly when that product breathes an air of trouble that might somehow settle on other consumer products they are putting out. Four years ago, Robert B. Walker, then president and chairman of the board of American Tobacco and presently board chairman and chief executive officer of American Brands, delivered, before a meeting of merchandisers called the Fourteenth Annual Marketing Conference, an oration entitled "What the Chief Executive Expects from His Top Marketing Man," in which he told his audience:

> The law of the marketplace, like Darwin's Law of Evolution, is change or perish. With the persistence of the scientist, we must probe for new concepts, new insights into consumer behavior, new marketing techniques. And with the courage of the explorer, we must be willing to turn from the old that is tarnishing to the new that sparkles with promise — whether it be marketing procedures, new products, or product improvements. There's a great difference between playing not to lose and playing to win — at American Tobacco we play to win. . . . Gentlemen, my assignment was "What the Chief Executive Expects from His Top Marketing Man." My answer is *results*.

And now American Tobacco is part of American Brands, and the company, with Walker still at the dual controls, is deep in the fruit-juice business as well as the tobacco business, and is planning to enter the soap and hand-lotion business. As time goes by, it may be that such big and increasingly diversified tobacco companies will choose to concentrate the greater part of their promotional energies on non-tobacco but equally profitable consumer markets whose annual rate of expansion can be made at least to match the annual growth rate of the population. It is true that in Britain, where cigarette commercials on television were banned in 1965, sales of cigarettes, after an initial drop, have increased by about two percent over a five-year period in spite of the ban, and that this increase has approximately matched the growth of the adult population of Britain. But the British and American cigarette-marketing experiences are not readily comparable, and television advertising and promotion never did play as big a role in Britain as it has played here. Considering that even with commercial television, into which the American tobacco industry has poured at least a billion and a quarter advertising dollars just since the time of the Surgeon General's report, the industry has failed to keep its sales increasing at the same rate as the adult population, the question arises how well the industry can maintain its economic position over the long run without this constant aural and visual bombardment of consumers by way of the home screen. Once the marketing of cigarettes falls below a certain threshold of profitability, a great deal of the promotional force that has been behind the selling of this product is likely to be dissipated. And without continuing high-pressure campaigns to make cigarette smoking appear socially acceptable and desirable, the place of the habit in American life may steadily decline.

In the meantime, people who in the past have not been associated with the exercise of much direct power in American life (statisticians, cancer scientists, public-interest lawyers, teachers, public-service advertising men) and a small number of senators, their staff people, and some conscientious public servants in regulatory or other agencies, persevering through years of discouragement, have slowly but tellingly gathered momentum. And this force has become sufficient to help reverse — against all the money and the machinery of mass persuasion and the commercial and political influence of a most formidable American industry, against the vast inertia of government, even against the habituation, reluctant or otherwise, of millions of regular smokers — the growth of a vast and, it once seemed, almost universally accepted and apparently ineradicable personal custom. Nothing quite like this large-scale change in personal behavior has ever been accomplished before in the history of the American consumer state. It may well be that the power inherent in these individual efforts on behalf of public health and against the merchandising of illusions bearing dangerous consequences is, collectively, a precursor of a far greater power now accumulating. To an increasing degree, citizens of the consumer state seem to be perceiving their ability to turn upon their manipulators, to place widespread abuses of commercial privilege under the prohibition of laws that genuinely do protect the public, and, in effect, to give back to the people a sense of controlling their own lives.

1970

4

Selling Death

After the TV Ban: The Switch to Print —
A Journalist's Protest

In the period preceding the removal, by act of Congress, of all cigarette advertising from radio and television at the beginning of 1971, spokesmen for various tobacco companies were insistent, in interviews with reporters, that the industry planned no undue increase in the amount of cigarette advertising in the press when the ban on cigarette commercials went into effect. Some weeks after cigarette commercials were taken off the air, I became interested in whether it seemed likely that the press, and in particular magazines, would abstain from taking advantage of this situation by soliciting or accepting, for profit, any additional print advertising for a product that has been shown in medical studies (which have been reported in the press itself) to be the leading cause of lung cancer among men and a significant contributing factor in premature death from coronary heart disease, emphysema, and a number of other diseases. I have also been interested in exploring the extent to which the tobacco manufacturers have felt themselves restrained, in planning their cigarette-advertising campaigns in the print media for the period after the ban on radio and TV cigarette commercials, by the realization that any excessive increase in the number of print ads they took out might provoke the Federal Trade Commission to take some kind of regulatory action, for example requiring health warnings to be displayed in all print advertising.

By any such standards of restraint, the behavior of the tobacco companies and the magazines alike after the ban on cigarette commercials went into effect was alarming. A prime example existed in the advertising pages of *Life*. In the fall of 1969, in response to a letter from Senator Frank E. Moss of Utah, attempting to determine the attitude of various publishers to accepting an increased volume of cigarette advertising after a cutoff of cigarette commercials from the air, Andrew Heiskell, the chairman of Time, Inc., publicly assured the senator that his company would continue to take cigarette ads but that it had no intention of accepting any "overwhelming" amount of cigarette advertising as a result of the TV cutoff. What happened since this assurance can be gathered by the fact that whereas the first three issues of *Life* in 1970 carried twelve-and-a-half pages of cigarette advertising, the first three issues of the same magazine in 1971, immediately after the ban on cigarette ads on TV went into effect, carried twenty-two pages of cigarette advertising — all of them in color. And a comparison of the number of ads carried in the February 5, 1971, issue of *Life* with that in the first issue in February of 1970, showed that the number of cigarette ad pages has jumped from two to eight.

On February 8, 1971, *Life* carried a full-page ad in the *New York Times* in praise of what it called "Life's Editorial Power." The ad asked, rhetorically, "Who else had the photo of the National Guard about to fire at the Kent State kids? The reminiscences of Nikita Krushchev? The 242 pictures of one week's American war dead in Vietnam?" It went on, "That kind of editorial excellence gives *Life* more impact than any other magazine. And gives your ad more impact than it can get anywhere else."

How can any responsible publishing corporation use a claim of editorial excellence to hold forth the unblushing assurance, applying in this case to cigarette manufacturers, that ads for a product, the use of which is officially recognized as a major cause of disease and death each year, would have "more impact" than anywhere else? If *Life,* which carried those "242 pictures of one week's American war dead in Vietnam," were to carry pictures of the number of American cigarette smokers who succumbed to lung cancer alone in the course of an average week, it would need not 242 pictures, but at least four times that number. How can any publisher – anyone – *make money* out of selling advertisements for a product that is known to cause death on a disastrous national scale year after year? The record of *Time* is no more encouraging than *Life* in this respect. The first three issues of *Time* for 1970 carried eight pages of cigarette advertising. The first three issues of the same magazine for 1971 carried a little less than 21 pages of cigarette advertising. And *Newsweek* is not much better than

Time. In the first three months of 1970, *Newsweek* scheduled 50 pages of cigarette advertising — an increase of 108 percent. And nobody could accuse the editors of *Newsweek,* any more than one could accuse the editors of *Time* and *Life,* of not knowing the facts about the causal relationship between cigarette smoking and lung cancer and other fatal diseases. Nor could the editors of *Look* claim innocence about the facts concerning cigarette smoking and disease. The fact that *Life* and *Look* are in financial trouble can hardly be viewed as an acceptable excuse for their trying to prop up their corporate health at the expense of the health of their readers.

With certain honorable exceptions, such as *Mademoiselle* and *Glamour,* two Condé Nast publications that, because they are meant to appeal to young women, have decided against taking cigarette advertising, the women's magazines as a whole are soliciting and accepting a new flood of cigarette advertising. What makes the use of this medium of advertising so particularly detestable is the knowledge that although women are less prone to lung cancer than men, the lung-cancer rate among women smokers in the last fifteen years has shown an alarming rise. Further, women, when they try to stop smoking, appear to have greater difficulty than men in breaking themselves of the habit. To counteract the trend among the smoking population generally toward cutting down on cigarette consumption, tobacco manufacturers are making great efforts to develop the market among women — in particular by putting out new brands of cigarette "imaged" in such a way as to seem particularly attractive in the female market. Huge sums have been poured into the promotion of new "women's" cigarettes such as Virginia

Slims, put out by Philip Morris, and Eve, which Liggett & Myers introduced in 1971 on a national scale with huge double-page color spreads in the major magazines of general circulation and in the women's magazines. The introductory ads for women were headed, "Farewell to the ugly cigarette. Smoke pretty. Eve." The accompanying copy went on, "Hello to Eve. The first truly feminine cigarette – It's almost as pretty as you are. With pretty filter tip. Pretty pack. Rich, yet gentle flavor ... Women have been feminine since Eve. Now Cigarettes are feminine. Since Eve." The ad was illustrated with a color picture of a woman's hand, amid wild flowers, holding a pack of Eve, and the pack design showed the head of an innocent-looking woman gazing out from a profusion of flowers and greenery depicted in mock-tapestry style. The deliberately contrived themes in this particular advertisement of innocence and of temptation, and an equally deliberate concealment, by the hand that is shown holding the package, of the message printed on the side, "Warning: The Surgeon General Has Determined That Cigarette Smoking Is Dangerous to Your Health," surely make this one of the most deceitful cigarette advertising campaigns yet devised.

What is perfectly clear from all this is that the legal measures that have been taken so far to bring some measure of governmental control over cigarette advertising are altogether insufficient to restrain the tobacco industry from huge advertising campaigns in the furtherance of what can only be regarded – considering what is known about the relationship between cigarette smoking and various diseases – as manslaughter on a massive scale. And the press as a whole has been undeterred from acting as co-conspirator in this manslaughter for the sake of whatever additional profits publishers have been able to seize as a result of the ban on cigarette commercials on the air. Obviously, some drastic action has to be taken to correct this situation. Under the Public Health Cigarette Smoking Act of 1970 the Federal Trade Commission is preëmpted until July 1, 1971 from prohibiting cigarette advertising or even from requiring that health warnings be plainly visible in all cigarette advertising; thereafter, if the FTC wishes to act in these respects, it must give Congress six months' notice of its intention to do so. This preëmption was inserted in the Act through the pressure of tobacco industry lobbyists, who calculated that any such moves by the FTC might be forestalled in Congress with the help of the tobacco industry and its commercial and political allies. Even if such moves against cigarette advertising by the FTC were permitted by Congress, the resulting delay of approximately one year in controlling or prohibiting cigarette advertising would certainly have a contributory effect on the scores of thousands of human fatalities that occur in this country each year as a result of cigarette smoking. Under the circumstances, it does not seem to me that the FTC is in a position to bring an effective end to the systematic promotion for profit of this clearly lethal product. Consequently, I suggest that the problem of cigarette advertising be placed under the jurisdiction not only of the FTC but also of the Food and Drug Administration, and that all cigarette advertising in this country be banned under the provisions of the Federal Hazardous Substances Act, which authorizes the FDA to ban or control the sale or promotion of substances that because of their toxicity are hazardous to public health. The toxic substances covered by the terms of the Hazardous Substances Act include those that are capable of causing harm to humans "through inhalation." This definition fits cigarettes and cigarette smoking quite precisely, and I believe that if the Food and Drug Administration does move promptly to place cigarettes and cigarette smoking under the provisions of the Hazardous Substances Act for the purpose of bringing the promotion of cigarettes under adequate federal regulation, the Federal Trade Commission would then also be able either to ban all cigarette advertising or to require that strong health warnings be prominently displayed in the cigarette advertising that is allowed.

1971

5

Formal Representations to the Food and Drug Administration

March 22, 1971

Dr. Charles C. Edwards
Commissioner, Food and Drug Administration
5600 Fishers Lane
Rockville, Maryland

Dear Dr. Edwards:

In recent weeks, as I pointed out in an article in *The New Republic* of March 27, 1971, there has been a most disturbing increase in the amount of cigarette advertising appearing in the print media. It is clear that this increase of such advertising in magazines of large circulation is attributable to the cigarette manufacturers' diversion of a considerable part of the $220 million in advertising expenditures that they have been prohibited by federal law from putting into cigarette commercials on television and radio into the print media for the purpose of promoting the sale and consumption of brands of cigarettes. So far this year some large-circulation magazines have doubled or more than doubled the amount of cigarette advertising they were carrying in a comparable period last year.

The complete and consistent failure of the cigarette industry to engage in any self-regulation in promoting a product that has been shown to be most harmful to health and indeed to cause death on a massive scale in this country makes it obvious that very vigorous action is required immediately by your agency in order to warn the public in unmistakable terms of the very great dangers to health and life itself of cigarette smoking.

Under the Federal Hazardous Substances Act, you are empowered officially to declare as hazardous any substance that is found to be toxic and that "has the capacity to produce personal injury or illness to man through ingestion, inhalation, or absorption through a body surface." I wish to point out to you that cigarettes and cigarette smoking have been shown beyond doubt to be toxic under the definitions of Section 2(g) of the Act in that they produce illness to man through inhalation and/or absorption via the entire respiratory tract. For reliable data on human experience concerning the effects of cigarette smoking I refer you to the findings of the Advisory Committee on Smoking and Health to the Surgeon General in 1964, and to "The Health Consequences of Smoking; a Report of the Surgeon General: 1971." The latter is described by the Surgeon General as "a comprehensive review of more than twenty years of research into the problem of smoking and health."

In summary, the conclusions of this report are that cigarette smoking is a significant risk factor contributing to coronary heart disease; that it is associated with increased mortality from cerebrovascular disease; that it is a likely risk factor in the development of peripheral vascular disease; that it is the most important cause of chronic obstructive bronchopulmonary disease in the United States; and that it increases the risk of dying from pulmonary emphysema and chronic bronchitis.

It concludes that cigarette smoking is the main cause of lung cancer among men and that the risk of lung cancer increases with the number of cigarettes smoked per day and diminishes with the cessation of smoking; and also that cigarette smoking is a cause of lung cancer among women.

It concludes that cigarette smoking is a significant factor in the causation of cancer of the larynx and the development of cancer of the oral cavity, and it cites experimental studies suggesting that tobacco extracts and tobacco smoke contain initiators and promoters of cancerous changes in the oral cavity.

It concludes that cigarette smoking is associated with cancer of the esophagus. It associates cigarette smoking with cancer of the urinary bladder among men. It suggests an association between cigarette smoking and cancer of the pancreas. It concludes that cigarette-smoking males have an increased prevalence of peptic ulcer mortality ratio.

It finds that maternal smoking during pregnancy exerts a retarding influence on fetal growth and finds "strong evidence" that smoking mothers have a significantly greater number of unsuccessful pregnancies due to stillbirth and neonatal death as compared to nonsmoking mothers.

Considering these appalling findings can there be any doubt that the Food and Drug Administration does have the duty immediately to classify cigarettes as a hazardous substance under the Federal Hazardous Substances Act?

Is it not strange that federal marshals acting on behalf of the F.D.A. should seize, as they did on March 8, 1971, 2,000 cases of two laundry detergents on the grounds that the detergents had toxic effects on skin, and thus were considered dangerous to human health under the Federal Hazardous Substances Act — but that at the same time the F.D.A. should be standing passively by and neglecting to classify as hazardous a substance — namely, cigarettes — that causes illness, disablement, and death in the American population on a huge and continuing scale? Can you name another substance the use of which is directly and causally connected, as inhaling cigarette smoke is, to seventy-five percent of the 60,000 deaths that the Surgeon General has estimated to occur in this country last year from lung cancer alone?

After long delay, your agency wisely decided to ban cyclamates as food additives because they had been found to be carcinogenic in experimental animals and in the avian species, and thus, by extension, to be potentially carcinogenic in man. Does it not appear almost grotesquely inconsistent that while banning cyclamates in the marketplace you should fail to lay the lightest regulatory finger on the pushers and peddlers of a product that has been shown beyond all doubt to exert, as cigarettes have, widespread carcinogenic and other effects in man?

A distinguished committee of the Royal College of Physicians and Surgeons, in their recent report "Smoking and Health Now," used the word "holocaust" to describe the effects of smoking on the health of the millions of smokers in Great Britain. I cannot but think you will agree that this is an equally appropriate description of the devastation to life and health currently being caused throughout this country by cigarette smoking.

In view of these grim facts I believe not only that you should promptly declare cigarettes to be a hazardous substance under the Federal Hazardous Substances Act but also that you should officially recognize that you have the authority to classify cigarettes as a banned hazardous substance, if necessary.

And since you have the authority to declare cigarettes to be a banned hazardous substance, it follows that you have the authority — whether or not you do actually register cigarettes as a banned hazardous substance — to impose strict and meaningful restraints upon all commercial programs and campaigns to promote cigarette smoking, both generically and by brand. Thus, it is my conviction that you have the clear authority and responsibility under the Federal Hazardous Substances Act to insure that tobacco manufacturers, their distributors, sales executives, and advertising agents are held strictly accountable to federal law and to standards set up by your regulatory agency for the manner in which they promote and sell so manifestly dangerous a product as cigarettes.

To recommend one specific regulatory step, I wish to say that I believe you possess the authority to require cigarette manufacturers, for the protection of public health, progressively to reduce the tar and nicotine content of new products. (I may observe that Senators Warren G. Magnuson and Frank E. Moss have long advocated this step-by-step reduction.) Aside from whatever reduction in existing risks to health may directly result from thus lowering the exposure of smokers to relatively high concentrations of tar and nicotine in cigarettes, there would be a further protective benefit to the health of smokers in such a move. The lower the content of tar and nicotine is in the cigarettes they smoke, the less irresistibly habituating cigarettes tend to be to many smokers. Thus the Food and Drug Administration, in vigorously asserting its powers under the Federal Hazardous Substances Act, could take a step that would have the effect of encouraging many heavy smokers to moderate their habit.

In the opinion of Dr. Daniel Horn of the National Clearing House for Smoking and Health, the process of switching from high to low tar and nicotine cigarettes represents, for many heavy smokers who wish to end their habit but have difficulty in doing so, a way station on the road to giving up the habit. And a regulatory program that would thus encourage people to reduce or stop the habitual inhalation of a product the use of which is associated with a high and frighteningly widespread risk of disease and premature death is surely in the public interest.

I am forwarding copies of this letter to Senators Warren G. Magnuson and Frank E. Moss.

Yours sincerely,
Thomas Whiteside

Rockville, Maryland 20852

April 20, 1971

Mr. Thomas Whiteside
72 Barrow Street
New York, New York 10014

Dear Mr. Whiteside:

Commissioner Edwards asked me to reply and thank you for your letter of March 22, 1971, concerning cigarettes.

The Federal Hazardous Substances Act does not authorize the regulation of advertising but is restricted to labeling (and banning). The Public Health Cigarette Smoking Act of 1969 prohibits label statements on cigarettes other than that specified therein.

We have maintained that Congress did not intend to cover tobacco under the Federal Hazardous Substances Act. However, if we were to determine that tobacco was within the meaning of "hazardous substance" the only course of action available would be a banning procedure. (Labeling and advertising would not be appropriate as noted above). Additionally, the dangers associated with tobacco would seem to indicate banning as the proper course of action were cigarettes made subject to the Federal Hazardous Substances Act. We think that banning this product is a matter to be determined by Congress and in fact, Congress has asserted itself in this area twice in the last several years.

Sincerely yours,
M. J. Ryan, Director
Office of Legislative Services

April 27, 1971

Dr. Charles C. Edwards
Commissioner, Food and Drug Administration
5600 Fishers Lane
Rockville, Maryland

Dear Dr. Edwards:

On March 22, 1971, I wrote you to point out that the F.D.A. was not doing its duty as a federal regulatory agency by its failure to classify cigarettes, the carcinogenic effects of which upon humans are notorious, as a hazardous substance under the Federal Hazardous Substances Act. I have now received a letter signed by Mr. M. J. Ryan, director, Office of Legislative Services for your agency, in reply.

I am addressing you directly once more because Mr. Ryan's reply is unresponsive to my specific representations. My letter did not propose that tobacco be declared a banned hazardous substance by your agency. It specifically requested that your agency declare tobacco to be a hazardous substance under Section 2(g) of the Federal Hazardous Substances Act, for the purpose of warning the public of the dangers to health of cigarette smoking. An actual ban on cigarettes is not a necessary accompaniment of such a declaration. But if your agency were to insist that it is necessary, you have discretionary power to hold such a banning procedure in abeyance provided that tobacco manufacturers conform to whatever hazard-lowering measures your agency may require for the protection of public health, e.g., the setting of maximum tar-and-nicotine content in cigarettes, both for the purpose of reducing the amount of certain known toxic substances in cigarettes and for the purpose of encouraging the reduction among many smokers of the habituating effect of cigarettes.

The failure of the F.D.A. to move promptly to correct its gross oversight and to move swiftly to protect public health by classifying cigarettes as a hazardous substance is, in my opinion, inexcusable.

To illustrate the extreme urgency of the need for the action I have requested, I would like to observe that during the month that has now elapsed since I called upon you to enforce the provisions of the Federal Hazardous Substances Act as they relate to cigarettes, a reasonable estimate of the number of people in the United States who have died of lung cancer alone as a direct result of cigarette smoking is 3,750. I wish to remind you that this is only a small part of the human toll brought about by the consumption of cigarettes; in my previous letter I have already summarized the current findings of the Surgeon General concerning the ominous association of cigarette smoking with a number of serious diseases other than lung cancer.

There are other considerations. In addition to the prolonged suffering and tragic deaths of those afflicted with cigarette-induced lung cancer, one must further consider the enormous diversion of hospital, radiation, and surgical facilities necessary to extend the survival time of lung cancer sufferers. The huge burden of this treatment must be borne by the already overburdened health care system in this country. And that means that many people suffering from diseases other than cigarette-induced lung cancer are bound to be deprived of the kind of care they should be obtaining. In the long run, the citizens most penalized by the diversion of health care facilities to lung cancer victims of cigarette smoking tend to be the poor. Thus, one evil bears in its train a whole variety of other evils. While these secondary problems may not be visible in the statistical tables concerning the relationship between smoking and lung cancer, they are just as real a part of the health consequences of cigarette smoking as are 75 percent of the lung cancer cases in this country.

In the meantime, what have the regulatory agencies of the

United States government been doing on behalf of public health to govern the promotion of these death-dealing products that are so assiduously and arrantly advertised to be a desirable part of a glowingly healthy and youthful life style? So far as your agency is concerned, I am forced to conclude that there is only one answer to the question: no regulatory, no preventive action of any practical kind whatever has been taken as these deaths continue.

In the six years that have elapsed since the Surgeon General's massive report on Smoking and Health, the total number of Americans who have died of cigarette-induced lung cancer is approximately ten times the number of deaths caused in August, 1945, by the dropping of the atomic bomb on Hiroshima.

Can it possibly be true that the lethal effects of even ten Hiroshimas, in the form of these ten silent holocausts in our very midst, cannot move the Food and Drug Administration to act to warn and protect the American people against the perpetuation of this horror? It seems incredible to me, given the unassailable facts officially made available to the nation by the Surgeon General himself, that a citizen should have to request the head of a federal regulatory agency to perform his duty to protect the American people from 45,000 agonizing, lingering deaths a year induced by the promotional efforts of the corporate pushers and hustlers of these particular carcinogenic products. Yet it does indeed appear that I must respectfully say to you once again, Dr. Edwards: Your manifest duty is immediately to declare cigarettes to be a hazardous substance under the terms of the Federal Hazardous Substances Act.

I am forwarding copies of this letter to Senators Warren C. Magnuson and Frank E. Moss.

Yours sincerely,
Thomas Whiteside

APPENDIX

Excerpts from

The Health Consequences of Smoking

A Report of the Surgeon General: 1971

U.S. DEPARTMENT OF HEALTH,
EDUCATION, AND WELFARE
Public Health Service

137

Preface

This report is a comprehensive review of more than 20 years of research into the problem of smoking and health. This research has been carried on under the sponsorship of many entities in this country and abroad, including governments, universities, private research institutions, voluntary health agencies, and the tobacco industry.

Seven years ago, an advisory committee to the Surgeon General was able to conclude that cigarette smoking is a serious hazard to health and is related to illness and death from lung cancer, chronic bronchopulmonary disease, cardiovascular disease, and other diseases. In the intervening years a great deal of new research has been completed; this has resulted in a growing understanding of the biomechanisms whereby cigarette smoking adversely affects the human organism and contributes to the development of serious illness.

It is encouraging that cigarette consumption in this country is declining. If this decline can be maintained, it will result in better health for our population and fewer deaths among those of our citizens who are in their most productive years of life.

Jesse L. Steinfeld, M.D.
Surgeon General

139

GENERAL CONSIDERATIONS

The first major development in the modern history of the effects of smoking on health occurred in 1950 with the publication of four retrospective studies on smoking habits among lung cancer patients and among controls. At that time, the question was, "Are smokers more likely to get lung cancer than nonsmokers?" Although some epidemiologists were satisfied that the answer was in the affirmative, others turned for confirmation to prospective studies in which the smoking habits of large populations were recorded and the populations followed to identify subsequent mortality. The first report in 1954 of Hammond and Horn showed significantly elevated overall death rate for smokers as compared to non-smokers. This elevation in death rates, almost entirely confined to those who smoked cigarettes, together with the evidence for a gradient according to the amount smoked, changed the question from one concerning only lung cancer to one concerning overall death rates and from one concerning smoking to one primarily concerned with cigarette smoking. In effect, the question became, "Do cigarette smokers have higher overall death rates than non-smokers and smokers of pipes and cigars?"

With the publication of the later reports of the major prospective studies in the late 1950s and 1960s, it became clear that cigarette smokers had higher overall death rates than non-smokers, as well as higher death rates from a number of individual causes of death. The question then became "Why?"

When the Advisory Committee on Smoking and Health to the Surgeon General was established in 1962, it undertook the evaluation of the scientific evidence up to that time. The conclusion of the Committee in its 1964 Report was that: "Cigarette smoking is a health hazard of sufficient importance in the United States to warrant appropriate remedial action." Not only did the Committee conclude that the evidence clearly showed that male cigarette smokers do in fact have higher death rates than non-smokers but that the convergence of epidemiological, experimental, and pathological evidence also clearly indicated a cause-and-effect relationship for several of the implicated diseases, particularly cancer of the lung and chronic bronchitis. In several other important diseases, the evidence of biomechanisms to explain epidemiological associations was felt to be inadequate at that time to draw firm conclusions about a cause-and-effect relationship.

Three and one-half years later, when *The Health Consequences of Smoking: A Public Health Service Review, 1967* was published, the conclusions of the 1964 review were taken as a starting point, and the nature of the task of interpreting the scientific evidence was restated as follows:

> How much mortality and excess disability are associated with smoking?
>
> How much of this early mortality and excess disability would not have occurred if people had not taken up smoking?
>
> How much of this early mortality and excess disability could be averted by the cessation or reduction of cigarette smoking?
>
> What are the biomechanisms whereby these effects take place and what are the critical factors in these mechanisms?

That, and subsequent reviews in 1968 and 1969, have provided some answers to these questions, particularly in summarizing the evidence for various theories as to how cigarette smoking affects the human organism to produce elevated disease and death rates.

At least five different processes have been suggested whereby cigarette smokers experience higher mortality or morbidity rates than do non-smokers.

1. Cigarette smoking *initiates* a disease process by producing progressive irreversible damage. In this case, the total effect would be approximately proportional to the total accumulated dosage experienced over the years. Cessation of smoking leaves impaired function which does not improve appreciably but does not continue to deteriorate from continued exposure to cigarette smoke. However, such function may deteriorate through aging or through exposure to other harmful agents. It appears that such a relationship probably exists for chronic obstructive lung disease and possibly for the development of atherosclerotic heart disease.

2. Cigarette smoking *initiates* a disease process with continual repair and recovery until some critical point is reached at which the process is

no longer reversible. The total effect would therefore be affected to some extent by accumulated exposure but would be affected also by the level of contemporary smoking. Cessation of smoking would result in a rapid reduction of risk provided the critical level initiating an irreversible process has nòt been reached. The evidence supports this kind of mechanism accounting both for the high dose-response relationship in lung cancer and for the reduction in risk from lung cancer among ex-smokers.

3. Cigarette smoking *promotes* a disease process either by providing positive support to the development of a pathological condition or by interfering with and diminishing the normal capability of the organism to cope with and defend against a disease process. This may take place by promoting the development of a subclinical disease to a clinically recognizable one, by promoting a mild disease state to a more severe form, or by increasing fatality rates of severe disease states. This type of mechanism could account for modestly increased mortality rates for a number of severe diseases for which there is no evidence that cigarette smoking itself has a role in initiating the disease. Some of the excess mortality from infectious respiratory disease and from coronary heart disease might take place through this kind of mechanism.

4. Cigarette smoking *produces* a set of temporary conditions which increase the probability that a critical event will occur with attendant disability and possibly fatal consequences. For example, there is evidence to support the theory that each cigarette can produce a set of conditions which increase the probability of myocardial damage through increased demand for oxygen at a time when the supply is diminished. Presumably, once the supply/demand imbalance is alleviated, the probability of myocardial damage would revert to its normal level. Cessation of smoking should have an almost immediate effect of reducing the risk sharply for morbidity or mortality produced through this mechanism.

5. Cigarette smoking may be artificially related to excess disability or death by way of a close association with some other condition or exposure which is found at a high level in smokers, but not in non-smokers, and is itself responsible for the disease. The one cause of death for which cigarette smokers have elevated death rates that is

generally interpreted in this way is cirrhosis of the liver. Since most heavy consumers of alcoholic beverages are smokers, and since alcohol consumption is an important part of the process that produces cirrhosis of the liver, the high rate of cirrhosis among cigarette smokers is discounted as resulting from this kind of artificial relationship. Some authors have proposed that there may be genetic factors that link smoking and certain diseases in this fashion. Obviously, the cessation of smoking would have no effect on morbidity or mortality from diseases which are artificially related to smoking.

These different ways in which cigarette smoking can be related to elevated morbidity and mortality rates are important considerations in attempting to estimate the potential public health benefits of giving up smoking. For some types of relationship, there would be no benefits; for some, rather small benefits; for some, substantial benefits, taking place over a long period of time; and for others, substantial benefits taking place rather rapidly.

During the past few years, a sharp reduction has taken place in the cigarette smoking habits of the U.S. population. The National Center for Health Statistics has recently published a comparison of smoking habits in the U.S. in 1955 and 1966 based on two large scale household surveys. These showed a drop in cigarette consumption in men under 55 years of age but no appreciable change among those 55 or over. Among women, every age group showed an increase in the eleven year period. A recent survey conducted for the National Clearinghouse for Smoking and Health, based on a much smaller sample (approximately 5,000 interviews), was conducted in the spring of 1970. Even with the smaller number of cases, it is clear that a much larger drop took place in the four years from 1966 to 1970 than in the eleven years from 1955 to 1966. The drop extended to the age group 55-64 among men, again with no appreciable drop among men over age 65. For the first time, the increase in smoking among women leveled off or even dropped slightly among women under 55. The increase among women over 55 was of a lesser magnitude than previously observed.

With the massive changes in smoking behavior which have taken place among adults in the past few years, largely as an expression of the desire to protect health, changes should be expected in mortality rates among those groups which have experienced the greatest reduction both in accumulated dosage and in concurrent dosage. An analysis of U.S. mortality rates for 1970 and the years to follow will provide a very valuable addition to the knowledge concerning the effects of smoking on death rates . . . .

SUMMARY OF THE REPORT

CARDIOVASCULAR DISEASES

Coronary Heart Disease

1. Data from numerous prospective and retrospective studies confirm the judgment that cigarette smoking is a significant risk factor contributing to the development of coronary heart disease, including fatal CHD and its most severe expression, sudden and unexpected death. The risk of CHD incurred by smoking of pipes and cigars is appreciably less than that incurred by cigarette smokers.

2. Analysis of other factors associated with CHD (high serum cholesterol, high blood pressure, and physical inactivity) show that cigarette smoking operates independently of these other factors and can act jointly with certain of them to increase the risk of CHD appreciably.

3. There is evidence that cigarette smoking may accelerate the pathophysiological changes of preexistent coronary heart disease which is already present and may contribute to sudden death from CHD.

4. Autopsy studies suggest that cigarette smoking is associated with a significant increase in atherosclerosis of the aorta and coronary arteries.

5. The cessation of smoking is associated with the decreased risk of death from CHD.

6. Experimental studies in animals and humans suggest that cigarette smoking may contribute to the development of CHD and/or its manifestations by one or more of the following mechanisms:

   a. Cigarette smoking, by contributing to the release of catecholamines, causes increased myocardial wall tension, contraction velocity, and heart rate, and thereby increases the work of the heart and the myocardial demand for oxygen and other nutrients.

b. Among individuals with coronary atherosclerosis, cigarette smoking appears to create an imbalance between the increased needs of the myocardium and an insufficient increase in coronary blood flow and oxygenation.

c. Carboxyhemoglobin, formed from the inhaled carbon monoxide, diminishes the availability of oxygen to the myocardium and may also contribute to the development of atherosclerosis.

d. The impairment of pulmonary function caused by cigarette smoking may contribute to arterial hypoxemia, thus reducing the amount of oxygen available to the myocardium.

e. Cigarette smoking may cause an increase in platelet adhesiveness which might contribute to acute thrombus formation.

Summary Statement of Recent Additions to Knowledge Relating Smoking and Coronary Heart Disease: A number of epidemiologic studies have provided additional evidence concerning cigarette smoking as a risk factor in the development of CHD. Experimental studies on animals have suggested that cigarette smoking, particularly the absorbed nicotine and carbon monoxide, contributes to the development of atherosclerosis . . . .

CHRONIC OBSTRUCTIVE
BRONCHOPULMONARY DISEASE

1. Cigarette smoking is the most important cause of chronic obstructive bronchopulmonary disease in the United States. Cigarette smoking increases the risk of dying from pulmonary emphysema and chronic bronchitis. Cigarette smokers show an increased prevalence of respiratory symptoms, including cough, sputum production and breathlessness, when compared with non-smokers. Ventilatory function is decreased in smokers when compared with non-smokers.

2. Cigarette smoking does not appear to be related to death from bronchial asthma, although it may increase the frequency and severity of asthmatic attacks in patients already suffering from this disease.

3. The risk of developing or dying from COPD among pipe and/or cigar smokers is probably higher than that among non-smokers, while clearly less than that among cigarette smokers.

4. Ex-cigarette smokers have lower death rates from COPD than do continuing smokers. The cessation of cigarette smoking is associated with improvement in ventilatory function and with a decrease in pulmonary symptom prevalence.

5. Young, relatively asymptomatic, cigarette smokers show measurably altered ventilatory function when compared with non-smokers of the same age.

6. For the bulk of the population of the United States, the importance of cigarette smoking as a cause of COPD is much greater than that of atmospheric pollution or occupational exposure. However, exposure to excessive atmospheric pollution or dusty occupational materials and cigarette smoking may act jointly to produce greater COPD morbidity and mortality.

7. The results of experiments in both animals and humans have demonstrated that the inhalation of cigarette smoke is associated with acute and chronic changes in ventilatory function and pulmonary histology. Cigarette smoking has been shown to alter the mechanism of pulmonary clearance and adversely affect ciliary function.

8. Pathological studies have shown that cigarette smokers who die of diseases other than COPD have histologic changes characteristic of COPD in the bronchial tree and pulmonary parenchyma more frequently than do non-smokers.

9. Respiratory infections are more prevalent and severe among cigarette smokers, particularly heavy smokers, than among non-smokers.

10. Cigarette smokers appear to develop more postoperative pulmonary complications more frequently than non-smokers.

Summary Statement of Recent Additions of Knowledge Relating to Chronic Obstructive Bronchopulmonary Disease: Studies have demonstrated that cigarette smokers show increased symptoms and pulmonary dysfunction as well as mortality from COPD when compared to non-smokers. Investigations of $alpha_1$-antitrypsin deficiency in relationship to pulmonary emphysema have suggested that cigarette smoking may act jointly with hereditary factors in the pathogenesis of pulmonary emphysema. A pathological study on animals have shown that long-term inhalation of cigarette smoke produces lesions characteristic of pulmonary emphysema.

CANCER

Lung Cancer

1. Epidemiological evidence derived from a number of prospective and retrospective studies, coupled with experimental and pathological evidence, confirms the conclusion that cigarette smoking is the main cause of lung cancer in men. These studies reveal that the risk of developing lung cancer increases with the number of cigarettes smoked per day, the duration of smoking, and earlier initiation, and diminishes with cessation of smoking.

2. Cigarette smoking is a cause of lung cancer in women but accounts for a smaller proportion of the cases than in men. The mortality rates for women who smoke, although significantly higher than for female non-smokers, are lower than for men who smoke. This difference may be at least partially attributable to differences in exposures: The use of fewer cigarettes per day, the use of filtered and low "tar" cigarettes, and lower levels of inhalation. Nevertheless, even when women are compared with men who apparently have similar levels of exposure to cigarette smoke, the mortality ratios appear to be lower in women.

3. The risk of developing lung cancer among pipe and/or cigar smokers is higher than for non-smokers but significantly lower than for cigarette smokers.

4. The risk of developing lung cancer appears to be higher among smokers who smoke high "tar" cigarettes or smoke in such a manner as to produce higher levels of "tar" in the inhaled smoke.

5. Ex-cigarette smokers have significantly lower death rates for lung cancer than continuing smokers. There is evidence to support the view that cessation of smoking by large numbers of cigarette smokers would be followed by lower lung cancer death rates.

6. Increased death rates from lung cancer have been observed among urban populations when compared with populations from rural environments. The evidence concerning the role of air pollution in the etiology of lung cancer is presently inconclusive. Factors such as occupational and smoking habit differences may also contribute to the urban-rural difference observed. Detailed epidemiologic surveys have shown that the urban factor exerts a small influence compared to the

overriding effect of cigarette smoking in the development of lung cancer.

7. Certain occupational exposures have been found to be associated with an increased risk of dying from lung cancer. Cigarette smoking interacts with these exposures in the pathogenesis of lung cancer so as to produce very much higher lung cancer death rates in those cigarette smokers who are also exposed to such substances.

8. Experimental studies on animals utilizing skin painting, tracheal instillation or implantation, and inhalation of cigarette smoke or its component compounds, have confirmed the presence of complete carcinogens as well as tumor initiators and promoters in tobacco smoke. Lung cancer has been found in dogs exposed to the inhalation of cigarette smoke over a period of more than two years.

Cancer of the Larynx

1. Epidemiological, experimental, and pathological studies support the conclusion that cigarette smoking is a significant factor in the causation of cancer of the larynx. The risk of developing laryngeal cancer among cigarette smokers as well as pipe and/or cigar smokers is significantly higher than among non-smokers. The magnitude of the risk for pipe and cigar smokers is about the same order as that for cigarette smokers, or possibly slightly lower.

2. Experimental exposure to the passive inhalation of cigarette smoke has been observed to produce premalignant and malignant changes in the larynx of hamsters.

Oral Cancer

1. Epidemiological and experimental studies contribute to the conclusion that smoking is a significant factor in the development of cancer of the oral cavity and that pipe smoking, alone or in conjunction with other forms of tobacco use, is causally related to cancer of the lip.

2. Experimental studies suggest that tobacco extracts and tobacco smoke contain initiators and promoters of cancerous changes in the oral cavity.

Cancer of the Esophagus

1. Epidemiological studies have demonstrated that cigarette smoking

is associated with the development of cancer of the esophagus. The risk of developing esophageal cancer among pipe and/or cigar smokers is greater than for non-smokers and of about the same order of magnitude as for cigarette smokers, or perhaps slightly lower.

2. Epidemiological studies have also indicated an association between esophageal cancer and alcohol consumption and that alcohol consumption may interact with cigarette smoking. This combination of exposures is associated with especially high rates of cancer of the esophagus.

Cancer of the Urinary Bladder and Kidney

1. Epidemiological studies have demonstrated an association of cigarette smoking with cancer of the urinary bladder among men. The association of tobacco usage and cancer of the kidney is less clear-cut.

2. Clinical and pathological studies have suggested that tobacco smoking may be related to alterations in the metabolism of tryptophan and may in this way contribute thereby to the development of urinary tract cancer.

Cancer of the Pancreas

Epidemiological studies have suggested an association between cigarette smoking and cancer of the pancreas. The significance of the relationship is not clear at this time.

Summary Statement of Recent Additions of Knowledge Relating Smoking and Cancer: Epidemiologic studies have confirmed that cigarette smokers incur an increased risk of dying from lung cancer and that those smokers who switched to filter cigarettes incur a lesser risk. Pathological studies have shown that cancer of the lung and cancer of the larynx have been found in animals exposed to the long-term inhalation of cigarette smoke.

SMOKING AND PREGNANCY

Maternal smoking during pregnancy exerts a retarding influence on fetal growth as manifested by decreased infant birthweight and an increased incidence of prematurity, defined by weight alone. There is strong evidence to support the view that smoking mothers have a significantly greater number of unsuccessful pregnancies due to stillbirth and neonatal death as compared to non-smoking mothers. There is insufficient evidence to support a comparable statement for abortions. The recently published second Report of the 1958 British Perinatal Mortality Survey, a carefully designed and controlled prospective study involving large numbers of patients, adds further support to the conclusions.

PEPTIC ULCER

Cigarette smoking males have an increased prevalence of peptic ulcer disease and a greater peptic ulcer mortality ratio. These relationships are stronger for gastric ulcer than for duodenal ulcer. Smoking appears to reduce the effectiveness of standard peptic ulcer treatment and to slow the rate of ulcer healing.

TOBACCO AMBLYOPIA

Tobacco amblyopia is presently a rare disorder in the United States. The evidence suggests that this disorder is related to nutritional or idiopathic deficiencies in certain detoxification mechanisms, particularly in handling the cyanide component of tobacco smoke.